This Book Is for You

☐ You want to enrich your daily spiritual practice.

☐ You want to know what the Jewish tradition has to say about sleep and dreaming.

☐ You have said the bedtime *Shema*—perhaps since you were a child—but you don't know what it means or what it can mean in your life.

☐ You're practicing Judaism, and you want to enhance your practice with a deeper level of spirituality.

☐ You have had difficulty sleeping or remembering your dreams.

☐ You're not Jewish, but you are curious about various aspects of Jewish spiritual practice and mysticism.

If any of these statements apply to you, you will want to delve into this book. You'll find here explorations of the meanings of traditional prayers that will surprise and enlighten you—and may even delight you. You will gain insights into sleep and dreaming. Your perception of your soul and your relationship to God will broaden and deepen. Most of all, if you integrate into your spiritual practice the concepts, movements, and meditations that are in this book, you will feel their effects in your life, in both sleeping and waking.

How to Use This Book

Don't worry about mastering all the information in this book immediately. We recommend you read it without trying to absorb everything, and that you then reread bits and pieces that attract you. Try the parts you like best from the prayers and meditations, work with them, and give yourself time to internalize the material.

We highly recommend that you spend about twenty minutes at night meditating or reading a prayer before you sleep. Do this for several nights before you add the next prayer or meditation. Eventually you will become accustomed to them, and the whole set of five prayers in the bedtime *Shema* will take about twenty minutes.

An abbreviated version of each prayer is at the end of the book (see p. 145). You can use these when you are too tired to say the full versions. Alternatively, on some nights you will want to spend a longer time with one prayer, and you can use the short version for the others.

This is a workbook for your spiritual growth, and you are the arbiter of how your spiritual growth develops. What we can tell you for certain is that if you use these prayers and meditations, you will deepen your life immeasurably.

We welcome your feedback, questions, and dreams. E-mail us at tfrankiel@juno.com or cgc1@aol.com; be sure to put "Temple of Dreams" in the subject line. Or write to us, care of Jewish Lights Publishing.

Entering the Temple of Dreams

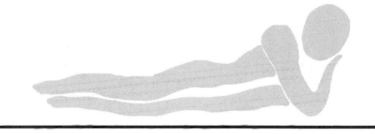

Jewish Prayers, Movements, and Meditations for the End of the Day

TAMAR FRANKIEL & JUDY GREENFELD

FOR PEOPLE OF ALL FAITHS, ALL BACKGROUNDS

JEWISH LIGHTS PUBLISHING ■ WOODSTOCK, VERMONT

Entering the Temple of Dreams:
Jewish Prayers, Movements, and Meditations for the End of the Day

Library of Congress Cataloging-in-Publication Data

Frankiel, Tamar, 1946–
    Entering the temple of dreams : Jewish prayers, movements, and meditations for the end of the day / by Tamar Frankiel and Judy Greenfeld.
            p. ;   cm.
    ISBN 1-58023-079-2
    1. Prayer—Judaism. 2. Meditation—Judaism. 3. Spiritual life—Judaism. 4. Gesture in worship. 5. Gesture—Religious aspects—Judaism. 6. Dreams—Religious aspects—Judaism. 7. Jewish meditations. 8. Judaism—Liturgy. I. Greenfeld, Judy, 1959–   II. Title.
    BM669.F64 2000   00-008095
    296.7'2—dc21   CIP

10 9 8 7 6 5 4 3 2 1

ISBN 1-58023-079-2 (Quality Paperback Original)

Manufactured in the United States of America
Cover design by Chelsea Dippel and Command Z
Text design by Chelsea Dippel
Photographs by Julian Hills, The Ant Farm
Illustrations by Angel Vernon

For People of All Faiths, All Backgrounds
Published by Jewish Lights Publishing
A Division of LongHill Partners, Inc.
Sunset Farm Offices, Rte. 4, P.O. Box 237
Woodstock, Vermont 05091
Tel: (802) 457-4000 Fax: (802) 457-4004
www.jewishlights.com

IN LOVING MEMORY of Ruth Jacobs Sizer (1917–1997) and Martha Darlington Jacobs (1875–1965).

—from Tamar

TO MY MOTHER, Belle Savransky, my greatest supporter.

—from Judy

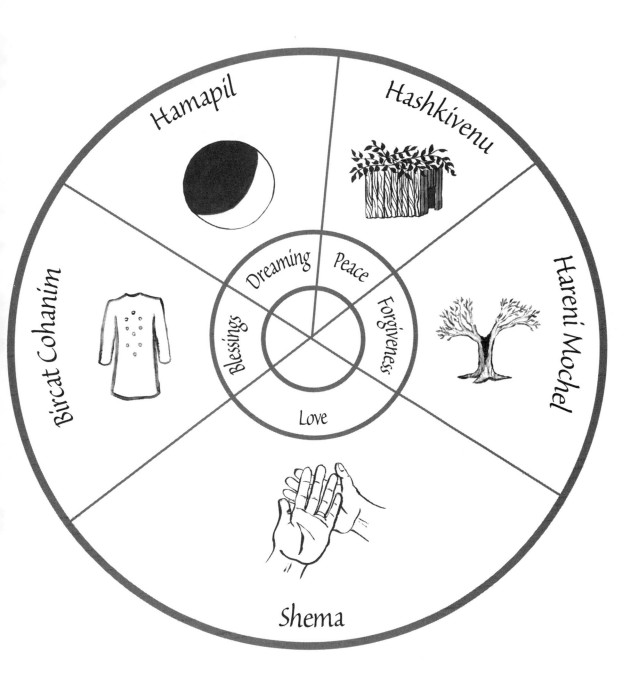

Prayer Wheel

Ending the Day with Blessings

Contents

5 ✹ *Bircat Cohanim:* Mighty Ones of Blessing—The Gift of Gavriel   100

6 ✹ *Hamapil:* Seeing in the Dark—The Gift of Uriel   122

The Bedtime *Shema:* Short Version   145

Preface

In our previous book, *Minding the Temple of the Soul*, we wrote about waking up in the morning and how to start your day with a spiritual focus. But we did not discuss another very important transition: going to sleep at night. As we have been teaching and working with people on their spiritual issues, questions have often arisen about this. Many people remembered, as one of their earliest spiritual moments, saying the bedtime *Shema* (pronounced "sh'mah") with their mothers or fathers. People also told us of difficulties they had sleeping and how they needed to close down the day in a meaningful way. They also asked us about dreams. Since we had been doing dream work and bedtime rituals for some time, this was the next step in the work we wanted to bring to readers.

Much to our surprise, when we began to do research on the bedtime *Shema*, it was difficult to find much commentary on it. Most of the standard commentators took for granted that night was a time of danger and demons, and that we had to protect ourselves from these dangers. While nighttime does bring fear, and almost all of us have had bad dreams, we wondered what positive things Jewish tradition might say about what happens at night. We knew, for example, that the Talmud regards dreams in a positive light. As we delved more deeply, we began to find in the mystical traditions, particularly those represented in the Zohar, the missing pieces we were seeking.

To our delight, once we began putting together the various segments of the Bedtime Prayers, we found that this ritual is indeed all of a piece. It takes us into a space of protection, clears our hearts and minds, and evokes the deepest layers of ourselves as we go into the world of dreams. In our rush toward fulfilling our material and technological aspirations, we have forgotten the profound significance of that world. We have forgotten the truths our ancestors knew, and neglected one of the crucial keys that will help return us to our Source—the world of night, moon, and dreams.

We are delighted to be among those helping to bring these truths back into our consciousness through the bedtime *Shema*.

This book would not have been possible were it not for the support, teachings, and insights we received from so many sources. First among them is our teacher and colleague Connie Kaplan, a woman of wisdom, compassion, and vision. From our Torah study circle, now in its sixth year of weekly meetings, we want to thank especially Toba August, Joyce Kirsch, and Randi Rose for their encouragement and interest. Our dream circle has nourished us for years as well and, although there are too many of you to thank individually, we must mention Jeanne Dancs, Ellie Farbstein, and Elaine Levi. Thanks to our students at Stephen Wise Temple who have studied with such enthusiasm.

Thanks to Randi Rose for reading an early draft of the manuscript; to our editor, Arthur Magida, for his most helpful comments and suggestions; and to Stuart Matlins, Sandra Korinchak, Emily Wichland, and all the staff at Jewish Lights who work toward success with such diligence and enthusiasm.

A special thanks to our families, who tolerated our long phone calls and meetings that were squeezed out of time they would have liked to have had with us. Thank you, Mike and Hershel; Samantha and David; Shmuel, Yaakov, Chava, Rina, and Devora—for supporting us, sharing your talents, and sharing your dreams. We are grateful as always for the continuing encouragement of our parents, Belle Savransky and John Sizer.

The Creation
of the
Sacred Dream

IN THE BEGINNING, God created a vast space for a dwelling place. God loved this *makom*, this sacred space, where Divinity could spread out in all its Glory. It was Good.

Eternities passed, and the magnitude of all this serenity and open space created a yearning, a desire to share this with another. The yearning that God did not know how to fill began to grow stronger and stronger, and it became painful. There was a Divine sadness because God did not know how to remedy this state of being. God began to withdraw into a void. This was *tzimtzum*.

One eternity, God fell into a very deep sleep and dreamed of four angelic beings who came and led God to a mirror. God gazed into the mirror and saw an image, which introduced itself as *Shekhinah*. As God watched, *Shekhinah* raised her hands and began to weave a most extraordinary vision. The *makom* began to fill with light and color that wove a new consciousness into God's reality. *Shekhinah* wove for him the dream of future worlds, of Creation, Formation, and Action, and of Wisdom, Beauty, Goodness, and Mercy. She wove the dream of the stars and planets, and the Divine order of the constellations. In the weave appeared Man, Woman, Child, the Jewish people, a Land, Torah, on and on through the frame of space-time until the weave was complete.

God was filled. The vision awakened such love and gratitude that God kneeled in front of *Shekhinah*. As the remnants of the weave dripped from her hands, God reached out and kissed them, then led her to join him for all eternities on the Throne of Glory. *Shekhinah* consented to unite with God beyond the worlds, so that together they could weave the Great Dream into manifestation.

As they stepped out of the Dream into the morning, their light created a great explosion. Billions of light fragments scattered above and spread over them like a wedding canopy as God and *Shekhinah* became the One. The heavens sparkled with joy at this grand union.

The Great Dream was born.

1

The "Other World" of Sleep

THINK OF THE TIMES you have sat before a beautiful sunset. As the sky changed and you sensed the beauty and awesomeness of the event, a calm and peace settled over you. Such a sight is a Divine gift. Now imagine that this sight came to you as a hint of yet another gift that comes with nightfall. Perhaps the radiance of red and orange and the deepening purple were calling to your imagination. The calm and peace that you felt at such a moment was speaking to your soul, asking you to go deeper into yourself. This is the call of the night, of sleep, of dreams.

It is sometimes difficult to answer that call by moving peacefully into sleep. The approach of sleep may be fraught with anxiety, and we do not settle into it completely. This uneasiness is virtually universal. All over the world, societies practice bedtime rituals—prayers, campfires, lullabies, the evening news—to help make the transition. Judaism has its own approach, a unique and powerful ceremony that can guide you from waking to sleeping. From the Jewish perspective, this is a special journey of the soul.

Interestingly, our sages said that "sleep is one-sixtieth of death" (Talmud *Berachot* 57b).[1] But death, in the rabbinic tradition, did not mean an end to life. Rather, death was a transition from the physical world into another world, the soul-world, which in its fullest expression was called *Gan Eden*, the Garden of Eden.[2] Sleep hints at that other reality, and dreams escort us into it. Similarly, the rabbinic saying that dreams are "one-sixtieth of prophecy" intimates that the deeper knowledge that comes to prophets also makes its appearance, at least to some degree, in dreams. This tells us that the death-like quality of sleep is certainly not a negative characteristic, although it is natural to have some trepidation about it. Somehow, the state of sleep, which brings dreaming-consciousness, allows a glimpse into a higher world that is beyond this one.

We will discuss this more fully in later chapters. In the meantime, we simply emphasize that what happens in sleep can be part of a full, spiritually conscious life. Dreaming has been devalued in our culture and reduced to a psychological tool for evaluating our mental health. In most traditional cultures, on the contrary, dreams are considered valuable because they have the potential to yield insight and information inaccessible to us in the waking state. Even in modern Western culture, many people, especially artists and scientists, say they receive inspiration or solutions to problems while asleep. Certainly the dreams recorded in the Bible—the dreams of Abraham, Jacob, and Joseph, for example—were regarded as very important. These examples suggest that we also can touch greater depths in our lives today through our own dreams.

The Soul as Night Traveler

Jewish mysticism explains the unusual state we refer to as "dreaming" as a change in the relationship between body and soul. To understand this, we must first become clear about what the soul is. The soul has no physical form, for its essence is identical with God. But we can imagine the soul as a beam of light that extends from its source in God to deep within the human body, pervading all its cells and extending beyond the body's physical boundaries. Using this model, body and soul are not opposites; rather, body is the densest form of spirit.

Beyond this, the soul has different levels or dimensions. The tradition of Kabbalah that we follow describes five levels of the soul:[3]

- ☐ *Nefesh*, the lowest level, maintains the life-force that enables the body to survive. The physical body is made up of trillions of cells, each with its multitudes of molecules, but it is the *nefesh* that gives these cells life and organizes them. The *nefesh* also includes our human instincts, such as the instinct for bonding with others, which is the basis for morality and a minimal sense of purpose. It is associated in the physical body with the lower torso and the center of gravity.

- ☐ *Ruach* is next. It is the level of soul that relates us to the larger world. A person's passion for self-expression stems from this level of soul. Our desire to dedicate our lives to something beyond ourselves is ultimately connected to the passion of the *ruach*. In the body, *ruach* is associated with the solar plexus, heart, and upper torso.

- ☐ *Neshamah* can see more broadly and deeply than the previous two levels. The *neshamah* operates on the mental plane. It is associated with the physical brain and is comfortable with abstractions. It can comprehend higher levels of unity, beyond the tangible and concrete world. Rabbi Moshe Chaim Luzzatto, an eminent mystical thinker who lived in the seventeenth century, explained that the *neshamah* is what the sages meant when they said, "Even though a person does not see [something], his *mazal* sees it" (Talmud *Megillah* 3a, *Sanhedrin* 94b), meaning one's *neshamah* has a perception beyond the ordinary senses.[4] Significantly, *mazal* is a term sometimes used for a guardian angel; it is also the term for one's zodiac signs.

- ☐ *Chayah* is the capacity for complete self-sacrifice to God. The level of consciousness that *chayah* represents extends beyond the individual; from it comes the possibility of a true collective consciousness (rather than a simple awareness of similarities and bonds, as with *nefesh*). *Chayah* makes possible a sense of unity with the Jewish people, the human race, other sentient beings, and a sense of *devekut*, or closeness with God. Its physical correlate is the space between the brain and the skull.

☐ **Yechidah** is totally united with the Divine. This is the level of the Divine spark in a person, the essence of the soul. *Yechidah* remains unaffected by mental, emotional, or physical circumstances. Physically, *yechidah* is correlated with the area above the fontanel. However, both *chayah* and *yechidah*, being beyond the individual, are often represented as metaphorically "surrounding" the body.

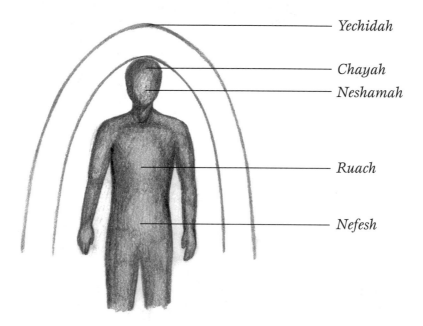

The Divine Soul as a unity is a source of life, protection, and guidance for the body. When we are awake, our active intellect, which is connected to the *neshamah*, keeps the idea of form and structure in place and allows the body and personality to continue existing. Moreover, the exercise of our moral will, which distinguishes good from bad and the permitted from the forbidden, maintains the boundaries of our world. At the same time, the *neshamah* also functions to connect us to spiritual realms.

In sleep, the higher parts of the soul loosen their ties with the body and extend like a long strand out into spiritual "space," leaving only the *nefesh* to guard the body. Then the soul is said to "travel" to other realms and have access to information beyond the normal parameters of waking consciousness.[5] This information comes into the brain encoded in images that make up our dreams.[6]

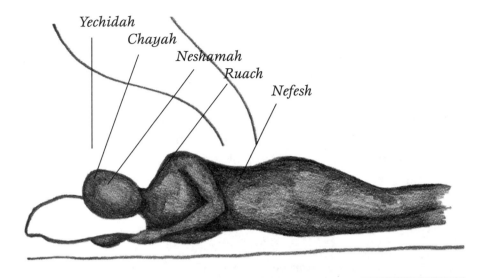

Yechidah
Chayah
Neshamah
Ruach
Nefesh

This soul-travel corresponds to specific physical occurrences that have been observed in sleep research. First, the rational, linear processing ability of the brain shuts down, including ordinary modes of perception of time and space. Sleep researchers call this "systematic cognitive withdrawal from the environment."[7] Second, in most dream states the body is paralyzed, so that the large voluntary muscles do not function. This is a great blessing because it probably prevents us from trying to act out what we are seeing in our dreams! Third, the brain experiences images that it records as visual, even though they do not result from light coming through the pupil of the eye onto the retina, as in ordinary sight.

But the most profound and powerful aspect of the change is that we must abandon conscious control of our lives. In order to sleep, we have to stop living our lives as we normally do. This can generate great anxiety and is particularly threatening to the ego, which is the part of our waking personality that keeps us oriented toward what we usually define as "reality." It is as if we defend ourselves against sleep because our waking consciousness—the ego that organizes perceptions of the external world, creates our self-image, and plans action—is instinctively regarded as essential for survival. Sleep brings another form of existence, one in which we cannot perceive, organize, or plan. Sleep demands surrender. The ego naturally resists. In fact, as sleep disorders demonstrate, the anxiety of the ego can be quite palpable.[8]

It is hard to let go and allow ourselves to experience the different sort of existence that occurs when we sleep. Our sages recommended the Bedtime Prayers as a cloak of protection and reassurance for the body and the ego. They provide a way to suffuse ourselves with trust and faith so our bodies can sleep and benefit from our soul's travels to other realms.

Yet there is more here than protecting the body while the soul travels. A different kind of consciousness arises when the ego releases its dominant hold on our reality. Traditionally, this consciousness is associated with darkness and the moon.

The Moon and the Night

The waking self can be compared to the sun and the sleeping self to the moon. The two are polar but complementary, like day and night. In Judaism, this was such an important polarity that it was compared to the two names for God in the Torah, Y-H-V-H (pronounced *Adonai*) and *Elohim*. As the Zohar states:

> "Know this day, and lay it to your heart that the Lord, he is God" (Deuteronomy 4:39). This means to combine the name *Elohim* with the name Y-H-V-H in the consciousness so that they form an indivisible unity.
> And this is the inner meaning of the text,
> "Let there be lights in the firmament of heaven" (Genesis 1:14).
> The omission of the letter *vav* from the word *me'orot* (lights) points to complete unity, to the black light and the white light being only two manifestations of one indivisible light.
> The same is symbolized by the "white cloud by day" and the "cloud of fire by night" (Exodus 13:21); the two phases of day and night are complementary to each other, both forming one whole, in order—as we read—to give light upon the earth.[9]

The sun and the moon were also considered complementary for, as the creation story says, these "two great lights" rule day and night (Genesis 1:14). The sun's significance is clear because its light and heat keep our basic life forces in operation. Yet the moon also is enormously powerful over events on earth. It rules the tides, which shape the life of the ocean and shoreline areas, as well as influence the climate.

Traditional agriculture sowed and cultivated plants according to the

phases of the moon. Ancient cultures paid attention to different qualities of different "moons" the year round. The Zohar cites a teaching that
"when the moon is dominant [i.e., full] ... all the lower heavens and
their hosts receive increased light, and the stars that have charge of the
earth all function and cause plants and trees to grow, and enrich the
earth, and even the waters and the fishes of the sea are more produc-
tive." [10] We should not be surprised if our own consciousness is at least
subtly affected by lunar phases. We might expect this to be the case
especially in sleeping consciousness, which the ego does not normally
control.

Even more than recognizing its physical influence, Jewish tradition
honors the moon as a spiritual symbol. Many aspects of Jewish ceremonial life are related to the moon:

☐ The Jewish calendar begins on a new moon (Rosh Hashanah).

☐ Two important holidays begin on the full moon—Pesach and
Sukkot. Also beginning on a full moon are the minor holidays of
Tu b'Shevat (the New Year of the Trees) and the currently
unobserved Tu b'Av, which celebrated the gathering of wood for
the Temple altars and was also a matchmaking holiday.

☐ Rosh Chodesh, the actual day that the new moon becomes visible in Jerusalem, is a minor holiday. On it, Jews say a version of
Hallel, a set of special praises to God, [11] and traditional Jews add
a *Musaf* (additional) service, with a Torah reading to commem-
orate the special sacrifice offered in the Jerusalem Temple on
Rosh Chodesh. It is regarded as a special holiday for women.
Traditionally, a special dish was prepared for Rosh Chodesh, and
women wore different clothing to mark the day. In modern
times, some women gather on Rosh Chodesh to learn Torah,
sing, and pray.

☐ Jews say a special prayer known as *Bircat Hachodesh*, the blessing of the new month, on the Shabbat before Rosh Chodesh.
This is traditionally inserted after the Torah reading in synagogue, while the scrolls are still out of the Ark.

☐ A special prayer is said during the waxing moon. This is known
as *Kiddush Levanah*, or sanctification of the moon. If possible,
it is said on Saturday night, immediately after the Shabbat that

falls in the second quarter of the lunar month. This is prefer-
able because people are still dressed in Shabbat clothes, which
add honor to the ceremony. However, if the moon is not visible
on that night, it can be said on a weeknight.

☐ In our mystical tradition, each month corresponds to one of the
twelve tribes of Israel, and each carries a different connotation
or meaning, similar to astrology.

Judaism's strong lunar consciousness suggests an appreciation of
the moon's power over processes of change. Indeed, the moon is the
epitome of impermanence because it changes its phase, then disappears and finally reappears. The sun, because it is the same day after
day, represents stability. On the other hand, the sun's seasonal changes
go to extremes—the dry heat of summer might be as dangerous as the
cold of winter. The moon, on the other hand, has a gentler, less fearful
pattern.

The Jewish sages said that the soul of the Jewish people can best be
understood in terms of the moon, rather than the sun.[12] The sun appears
in a blaze of glory, but at night it disappears completely. The moon can
be seen to grow small and large, day after day and night after night, but
it always returns to fullness. The sages saw the history of the Jewish
people in terms of the symbolism of the waxing and waning moon.
According to this symbology, the hot, bright sun represents the other
nations, which make their mark on earth with power and splendor.
Israel is the small light, which appears in its glory only after the sun
has set. This will be the fulfillment of the messianic prophecy that "the
light of the moon shall be as the light of the sun, and the light of the
sun sevenfold as the light of the seven days. On that day, when the Lord
shall heal the bruise of his people and the wound of its hurt" (Isaiah
30:26).[13]

The spiritual level of the Jewish people is also implied in this symbolism: When we are on the "downward" cycle of history, we are also
further from God. This is represented by the waning moon. However,
when we are in a good relationship with God, the moon waxes and,
symbolically, is restored to its fullness. Such "fullness" occurred during
the era of the patriarch Jacob, on Mount Sinai when Israel received the
Torah, and at the time of the building of the Temple by King Solomon.
The Zohar says:

> When Abraham appeared in the world he embraced the moon and drew her near; when Isaac came he took fast hold of her and clasped her affectionately, as it says: "His left hand under my head" (Song of Songs 2:6). But when Jacob came the sun joined the moon and she became illumined, so that Jacob was found perfect on all sides, and the moon was encircled in light and attained completion through the twelve tribes.[14]

Here too, it is understood that the moon will attain completion once more in messianic times.[15]

Comparing the Jewish people to the moon also explained Israel's smallness and apparent insignificance. This idea found its classic expression in a well-known *midrash* (contemporary interpretation of ancient biblical text) on the "diminishing of the moon." According to this midrash, after creating the sun and moon as the "two great lights," God diminished the moon so that the sky had "the big light and the small light." The moon complained, and God explained to her that even though she was smaller, she would rule by day as well as by night (the moon is also visible in daytime). Moreover, the Jewish people would rely on her to calculate their days and years. The moon raised more questions, and God replied that some of the greatest people in history would be called "the Small"—Jacob, the sage Samuel, and even King David. Finally, God asked to have an atonement sacrifice brought to the Temple for God on Rosh Chodesh because God had "sinned," apparently by diminishing the moon without her consent.[16]

One way of reading this midrash is to reassure the Jewish people that everything is in God's hands, and history will eventually turn in their favor, even if they are small today. Even more important, God was teaching the moon about the power that is hidden in what is small. God might have also reminded the moon of the Maccabees, who would overthrow a great power even though they began as just a band of guerrillas. Elijah heard God not in fire and earthquake, but in a "still small voice" (1 Kings 19:12). And at the beginning of the Jewish people's history, Moses himself had said, "It was not because you were more numerous than any other nation that the Lord cared for you and chose you, for you were the smallest of all nations" (Deuteronomy 7:7). But in that apparent insignificance, amazing things can be hidden. Greatness is not measured by size.

There are two kinds of illumination, "two great lights." One is that of

The Diminishing of the Moon: A New Story

One night when Levanah, the Elder called "Moon," was addressing her evening council of stars, she was asked to tell a story from her youth. "How did you learn to use the power of your grand moonlight?" one of the stars asked.

"Ah," said Levanah, "the power of the moonlight is that it sometimes hides and sometimes appears in its fullness." "But if you hide," objected one of the stars, "how can anyone see you? How can you even be sure you are having any effect on the universe when you are hiding?"

"When I was a very young moon," she said, "I also thought that strength lay in the power of brightness and intensity, like the sun. The sun every day was seen and felt by every creature. They talked about him, how he warmed them and lit up the day. I assumed he was better than I, because everyone saw him. Days were governed by sunset and sunrise. Plants grew toward sunlight. My light was barely noticed when the great sun was out; and at night most creatures were asleep and didn't see me.

"Frankly, I was envious. I grew despondent and angry. I decided to withhold my light. Every night I just peeked out a little. God noticed and came to talk to me. I have to say, God's face was stern.

"'I'm growing impatient with you, Levanah,' God said. 'You are being led astray by your eyes. You must see what I am going to show you now.' God pulled me out and made me shine in my full glory. Suddenly the oceans began to move toward me. Through the special vision I was given at that time, I could see the roots of the plants under the earth moving and spreading. I could see inside human beings, watching the fluids of their bodies and even their souls respond to my light.

"'What is this?' I exclaimed in astonishment.

"God replied, 'Your power is incredible. You have the strength to be a partner to the sun by day and a ruler by night. You guide plants, animals, and people with an internal compass. And the Jewish people, who are very special to me, will recognize this and set their calendar by your movements. Surely you would not pout if you could see yourself in your own unique truth.'

"I was speechless. I felt a deep humility and, at the same time, the beginnings of a sense of my own authentic being. I bowed to the Creator in humble gratitude. 'Forgive me,' I said, 'for not seeing my own gift and for looking at others in envy.'

"That is how I learned the lesson of subtlety and hidden strength."

The stars blinked in their wide-eyed way. As they went out to shine that night, they remembered how easy it was to be tempted to feel envious of others' gifts and miss their own. That night each star became a little more aware of its own uniqueness, thanks to the lesson of Levanah, the Elder of the Night: How to find greatness in what is small or even invisible to the eye.

the sun, whose large, intense light makes everything manifest and clear, so that the ordinary world appears to have solid reality. This is also the light of *mitzvot*, doing and accomplishing, bringing into action what the Torah says. The Zohar compares this to the work of Abraham: "'And Abraham was old, advancing in days' (Genesis 24:1)—that is, in illumination, and as he grew older his light continued to expand, so that he was 'shining more and more to the perfect day' (Proverbs 4:18)."[17]

The other light appears to be absence of light, but it is really the "black light"—the darkness, the world of dreams. Mystically, this is represented by Isaac, as the Zohar again explains: "'The darkness' is a description of Isaac, who represents darkness and night, and hence when he was old his eyes were dim, so that he could not see. He had to become enveloped in darkness in order to become attached to his own proper level…until to him could be applied the words, 'And the darkness He called night.'"[18] Similarly, the "dark night of the soul" is a classic metaphor. What it represents is a descent into uncertainty that is so deep it is like trying to find one's way in complete darkness, but from that experience we can learn to live on another plane.

King David is a great hero of Jewish tradition—poet, soldier, and king—who is associated with darkness and the moon. The Zohar tells us that he called God "Midnight."[19] He was from the side of darkness, like Isaac, and "had no light of his own." According to an ancient midrash, his original destiny was that he would die at birth. But when Adam saw that such a great soul would have no life, he gave him seventy years of his own. The Zohar adds that Abraham, Jacob, and Joseph contributed some of their years to enrich that seventy.[20] Thus David, who in Kabbalah represents the *sefirah* called *Malkhut* (Kingship, the tenth of the *sefirot*), was the ultimate receptive person, like the moon. Yet he brought into the world poems that would light up the ages, and a messianic consciousness that would sustain the Jewish people's faith in the future.

From the sun's point of view, the moon's light is "only" a reflection. It "has no light of its own." But the moon has a special light. It has charm and grace, even though it does not have the sun's warmth. Life on earth would not be possible without the sun, but it would also not be possible without the moon causing the movement of tides and waters. Similarly, some things can be accomplished in waking consciousness, but other things can be accomplished only in dreaming consciousness.

While awake, we can give solidity to our ideas; while asleep, we can create anew.

When the moon lights the night, we can see in the darkness, even though this seeing is different from that of the day. The prophecy that "the light of the moon shall be as the light of the sun" is not merely an allusion to a future ideal history. It is also a metaphor for a new understanding that is about to emerge in human thought: that the quality of consciousness associated with moon, night, and darkness has deep and permanent value. Part of our spiritual work is to illumine the darkness just as the moon does when it is full.

We carry a reminder in our bodies of the light of the moon, as this midrash relates:

> When Adam and Chava were created, the light was so bright and the air so clear that they could see from one end of the world to the other. They were of incredible beauty, and their skin shone like the petal of a lily in the moonlight. After they ate of the fruit of the tree, God put away the light, to be revealed again at the end of days. However, God allowed a tiny portion of that light for each home on Friday night, when candles are lit for Shabbat.
>
> God also made garments for Adam and Chava, to replace the translucent white skin that disappeared. Only a small portion of it was left, at the base of the fingernails, which we call the "moons."

On Saturday night when we end Shabbat with the *Havdalah* service, we look at those moons and remember that we truly reflect the Divine. But we do not need to wait until *Havdalah* for that reminder. We can have that same realization each night as we enter our dreams.

Recovering the Sweetness of Sleep

Just as the moon is sometimes seen negatively, sleep also is sometimes seen as a spiritually negative state. This is a limited viewpoint, but some of its proponents have been prominent in Jewish tradition. They hold that waking consciousness is "expanded consciousness" (although one can also be spiritually "asleep" during the day!) and sleep is "constricted consciousness." [21] Accordingly, one should sleep as little as possible. The saintly person (a *tzaddik*) in Judaism has been described as "the one who is constantly consumed by love for God to the extent that he is unable to sleep at night, so agonized is he by the fear of losing conscious contact with the Beloved." To minimize sleep was frequently upheld as the ideal, because for a holy person, the "expanded consciousness and the holy thoughts of the whole day disappear, and on the following day you have to begin again and make great efforts to regain that level once again." Of course, such a person didn't stay up late just to run a business; the purpose was to learn Torah or say prayers. As a result of this spiritual tradition, many devout Jews have the custom of rising at midnight to say psalms and/or to pray for the restoration of Jerusalem and the Holy Temple; this is called *Tikkun Hatzot* (Mending [the World] at Midnight).[22]

This viewpoint is based on two traditions: one from the Talmud, which says that King David's harp woke him at midnight to sing God's praises; and a later one from the mystics, which states that holy souls join with God at midnight. The Zohar mentions both:

> Every night the souls of the righteous mount on high, and at the hour of midnight the Holy-One-Blessed-Be-He comes to the Garden of Eden to disport himself with them.
>
> With which of them? Rabbi Jose says, with all—both those whose abode is in the other world, and those who are still in their dwellings in this world ....
>
> At midnight all the truly righteous arise to read the Torah and to sing psalms, and we have learned that Holy-One-Blessed-Be-He and all the righteous in the Garden of Eden listen to their voices .... Hence it is that the praises that are sung at night constitute the most perfect praise.
>
> See now, King David too used to get up in the middle of the night .... He did not remain sitting or lying in his bed, but he literally rose and stood up to compose psalms and praises .... He, as it were, awoke the dawn, as it is written, "Awake, my glory, awake, songs and harp; I myself will awake very early" (Psalms 57:9).[23]

It would seem that the less sleep the better, so long as the nocturnal waking hours are spent in prayer. Yet rabbinic advisers did not recommend this for an ordinary person. Holy individuals, who had disciplined their passions and devoted virtually all their time to study and prayer, could do with little sleep because they did not expend energy in the same emotional struggles as the ordinary person did, and did not need to recover that energy in sleep. Some sages also felt that the tradition of staying awake might easily go too far. As one great rabbi said, a person should have "his mind clear and bright and undimmed, and his body vigorous .... Staying awake too much is very harmful."[24]

We follow a different rabbinic viewpoint: that we can actually do spiritual work while sleeping. For example, the Hasidic Rabbi Tzvi of Ziditchov said that if he accomplished in sleep only what he does while he is awake, it was not a good sleep. In his view, the service of God during sleep could—and should—be higher than during waking hours, because the soul is then freed from the body. The great Rabbi Chaim of Volozhin said that his teacher, the famous Vilna Gaon, had stated that God created sleep so that we could attain insights that were unattainable in our waking state. Some of our greatest teachers—including the Baal Shem Tov, who was the founder of Hasidism, and Joseph Caro, the great legal scholar—were taught by spiritual beings in their sleep.[25]

From this perspective, we sleep so we can dream, and dreams are ways to heal and sources of information. If we sleep well—whether for short or long periods, and in accordance with our own patterns and with the sort of spiritual preparation provided by the Bedtime Prayers—sleep is not spiritually negative or neutral. It is positive. The Zohar illustrates this with a story of Rabbi Isaac, who went to Rabbi Yehudah despondent because he expected to die soon. Rabbi Yehudah asked him why he thought so. Rabbi Isaac responded, "My soul has lately been leaving me in the night and not enlightening me with dreams as it used to do."[26] Dreams are part of living fully the soul's life on earth.

> "With my soul have I desired You in the night, yea, with my spirit within me will I seek You early" (Isaiah 26:9). Rabbi Shimon said, "The inner meaning of this verse is as follows: When a man lies down in bed, his soul leaves him and begins to mount on high, leaving with the body only the impression of a receptacle that contains the heartbeat. The rest of it tries to soar from grade to grade, and in so doing it encounters certain bright but unclean essences. If it is pure and has not defiled itself by day, it rises above them ... and there they show her certain things that are going to happen in the near future. (Sometimes they delude her and show her false things.) Thus she goes about the whole night until the man wakes up, when she returns to her place. Happy are the righteous to whom God reveals secrets in dreams! ...[27]

If God joins the souls of the righteous in the heavenly ceremonies at midnight, we do not all have to awaken ourselves to join them. If our souls are ready, they can travel to the Garden while we are asleep. We will bring back their messages in our dreams. That allows the imagination, guided by the soul, to bring potential into form. This literally brings light from darkness.

Sleep, then, is not only physical rest for the brain but also an opportunity for the soul. The record of that work is our dreams. But the transition from daytime, or "sun" consciousness, to nighttime, or "moon" consciousness, can be troublesome and requires preparation. It is comparable to preparing for a journey to a special place of quiet and repose, or to preparing for Shabbat, which brings an end to our work week so we can withdraw into a more spiritual state. Like these, sleep needs our attention, particularly if the ego resists it.

Nothing is more appropriate for this than a bedtime ritual that helps the mind shut down peacefully. Sleep experts recommend that a person repeat the same thing every night and use rituals with words, songs, and rhythms that are repetitive and relaxing.[28] The Jewish Bedtime Prayers do this, but their additional content guides our souls to the Divine Light that comes through in the night.

A Ceremony for Dreaming: *Shema al Mitah*

Shema al Mitah literally means saying "the *Shema* on one's bed." This is loosely referred to as the Bedtime Prayers. The saying of the *Shema* and perhaps the *Hamapil* (the final prayer of the bedtime *Shema*) goes back 2,500 years, when the judicial group known as the "Men of the Great Assembly" (*Anshe Knesset HaGedolah*) began to establish set prayers after the Jewish people started to return to Israel from their exile in Babylon. According to this tradition, the first two paragraphs of the *Shema* should be said at bedtime (but not the third paragraph, which has to do with the daytime practice of wearing *tzitzit*, or fringes). In addition, the blessing *Hamapil* should be said on retiring (*Berachot* 60b). The Talmud also says that even if we have fulfilled the *mitzvah* of saying the *Shema* by praying the *ma'ariv* (Evening Service), we should still say it again at bedtime (*Berachot* 4b).[29]

Other parts of the Bedtime Prayers were added at different times. The *Hashkivenu*, which appears in the *ma'ariv* and is imported into the Bedtime Prayers, is probably from Talmudic times (400–600 C.E.).

The Prayer of Forgiveness apparently dates from medieval times, although it may go back to Talmudic traditions. The very ancient Priestly Blessing and other verses found in the different versions were inserted sometime between the era of the Talmud and the late medieval period.

Slightly different versions of the *Shema al Mitah* appear in different *siddurim* (prayerbooks), but all are designed to be said in the privacy of our bedrooms just before sleep. Because the Bedtime Prayers were never used in the synagogue or associated with the ancient Temple services, they retained greater flexibility than the regular services. These are not the only things that can help prepare us for sleep. It is also recommended that we study something from Jewish tradition before going to bed— an *aggadic* (story) portion of the Talmud, a Hasidic story, or the Zohar.[30] But the prayers provide the ceremonial structure that guides our intent, as we will show in the following chapters.

In our compilation of prayers, we have used five basic components found in most prayerbooks, with a slightly different order and some variations in wording:

- ☐ ***Hashkivenu***: "Lay us down," from the *ma'ariv*, or Evening Service, in the synagogue.

- ☐ ***Hareni mochel***: "I am ready to forgive, ..." the Prayer of Forgiveness.

- ☐ ***Shema***: the first paragraph. (Some versions of the *Shema al Mitah* use two paragraphs. See Appendix A for full text of the *Shema*.)

- ☐ ***Bircat Cohanim***: the Priestly Blessing from the Book of Numbers, a biblical verse commonly found in the various versions of the Bedtime Prayers. This blessing occurs frequently in Jewish life, and it has some interesting connections to sleep and dreams.

- ☐ ***Hamapil***: a blessing thanking God for sleep and illumination, after which no further words are spoken and we drift into sleep.[31]

In the following chapters, we will explain each of these prayers and suggest meditations and movements to accompany them.

הַשְׁכִּיבֵנוּ יהוה אֱלֹהֵינוּ לְשָׁלוֹם,

וְהַעֲמִידֵנוּ מַלְכֵּנוּ לְחַיִּים.

וּפְרוֹשׂ עָלֵינוּ סֻכַּת שְׁלוֹמֶךָ.

וְתַקְּנֵנוּ בְּעֵצָה טוֹבָה מִלְּפָנֶיךָ.

וְהוֹשִׁיעֵנוּ לְמַעַן שְׁמֶךָ. וְהָגֵן בַּעֲדֵנוּ,

וְהָסֵר מֵעָלֵינוּ

אוֹיֵב דֶּבֶר וְחֶרֶב וְרָעָב וְיָגוֹן.

וְהָסֵר שָׂטָן מִלְּפָנֵינוּ וּמֵאַחֲרֵינוּ.

וּבְצֵל כְּנָפֶיךָ תַּסְתִּירֵנוּ.

כִּי אֵל שׁוֹמְרֵנוּ וּמַצִּילֵנוּ אָתָּה,

כִּי אֵל מֶלֶךְ חַנּוּן וְרַחוּם אָתָּה.

וּשְׁמוֹר צֵאתֵנוּ וּבוֹאֵנוּ לְחַיִּים וּלְשָׁלוֹם,

מֵעַתָּה וְעַד עוֹלָם.

בְּשֵׁם יהוה אֱלֹהֵי יִשְׂרָאֵל

מִימִינִי מִיכָאֵל   וּמִשְּׂמֹאלִי גַּבְרִיאֵל

וּמִלְּפָנַי אוּרִיאֵל

וּמֵאֲחוֹרַי רְפָאֵל

וְעַל רֹאשִׁי שְׁכִינַת אֵל

Lay us down, Adonai our God, in peace,
and raise us up, our Ruler to life.
Spread over us a sukkah of Your peace
and set us right with good counsel from You.
Save us for the sake of Your Name,
shield us and remove from us
enemies, plague, sword, famine, and woe.
And remove spiritual impediment
from before us and behind us,
and shelter us in the shadow of Your wings.
For You are God who protects and rescues us,
for You are God the gracious and compassionate Ruler.
Safeguard our going and our coming, for life and peace,
now and forever.

———————

In the Name of Adonai, God of Israel:
May Michael be at my right   Gabriel at my left,
Uriel before me,
and Rafael behind me;
and above my head the Shekhinah of God.

2

Hashkivenu: Meeting with the Angels

JACOB SET OUT from the Well of the Oath and went on his way toward Haran. He came to a certain place and stopped there for the night, because the sun had set. Taking stones there, he made a pillow for his head and lay down to sleep. He dreamed that he saw a ladder that rested on the ground with its top reaching to heaven, and angels of God were going up and down upon it.

The Lord was standing beside him and said, "I am the Lord, the God of your father Abraham and the God of Isaac. This land on which you are lying I will give to you and your descendants. They shall be countless as the dust upon the earth, and you shall spread far and wide, to north and south, east and west. All the families of the earth shall pray to be blessed as you and your descendants are blessed. I will be with you, and I will protect you wherever you go and will bring you back to this land; for I will not leave you until I have done all that I have promised."

> Jacob woke from his sleep and said, "Truly the Lord is in this place, and I did not know it." Then he was awestruck and said, "How awesome is this place! This is no other than the house of God, this is the gate of heaven." Jacob rose early in the morning, took the stone on which he had laid his head, set it up as a sacred pillar and poured oil on the top of it. He named the place House of God.
>
> —Genesis 28:10–19

Protection on Our Journeys

In the famous dream of Jacob and the angels, he discovered that God was with him even when he left his home. God promised to protect him during all his journeys. This is the first theme of the Bedtime Prayers, reminding us that God is with us as God was with Jacob, and that angels accompany us on our nighttime journeys. The prayers begin with *Hashkivenu*, an expression of reassurance as our egos face the anxiety of the night.

The *Hashkivenu* is imported into the bedtime *Shema* from the *ma'ariv*, or Evening Service. Part of the prayer asks for protection from physical enemies, disease, hunger, and attacks by wild beasts. It also asks for the removal of "spiritual impediment from before us and behind us." The word that is translated "spiritual impediment" is *satan*, which medieval literature personified as a demon or devil, but which literally means "obstacle."[1] The prayer, then, refers to obstacles that are moral or spiritual in nature.

Spiritual obstacles arise in our daily life when we have difficulty making the right ethical or spiritual decisions. Traditionally, such obstacles were called "temptations"; today, they often take the form of social pressures. But what relevance does this have at night, when we are going to sleep and do not have the capacity or opportunity to make moral choices? Jewish mysticism understood that the time of sleep exposed people to dangers that they might be unaware of. If we had done something wrong during the day and not corrected it, or if we had had negative thoughts, those actions and feelings might still affect us at night. Like a kind of fallout, this negative energy could "eat away" at us when our minds are asleep. Rabbi Abraham Isaac Kook described this as follows: "When a person sleeps, the mental power departs from him, and he is left with the physical portion alone. The spirit of impurity rests on him and it can undermine the power of the physical alone, in time of sleep, to bring negative characteristics into him, even after he awakens."[2]

The "spirit of impurity" is the *satan* that the prayer mentions. This is the residue of energy created by our own actions. Of course, no one is perfect, and we should not expect that we can completely purify ourselves on any given day. Precisely because of this, the Bedtime Prayers offer a request for spiritual protection against the damage we might have unknowingly done to ourselves.

Besides our own deeds, there are also negative influences in the environment at large. Like second-hand smoke or environmental pollution, these influences do not originate from our own deeds or thoughts, but they can affect us. Neighborhoods where violence is common or where people are extremely materialistic create their own spiritual debris that affects even people who are not involved in such activities. These influences increase at night. Rav Kook describes them as "haters of the soul" and asserts that saying the Bedtime Prayers separates us from them like a shield of armor.[3]

Further, the *Hashkivenu*, by creating a protective shield, also provides a channel through which blessing can flow. Jewish mysticism hints at this in the traditions concerning the Evening Prayer, from which the *Hashkivenu* is taken. According to the Zohar, when Jacob originated the Evening Prayer by praying at night before lying down, he restored the light of the moon—that is, the light of the Jewish people: "Now Jacob desired to institute Evening Prayer and so restore the light of the moon and water her and enrich her with blessings on all sides." Moreover, the Evening Prayer joined the morning and afternoon prayers (inaugurated by Abraham and Isaac) to create three "legs" for the Divine Throne. This provided the firm support needed for the emanation of Divinity into the world.[4]

The *Hashkivenu* is like an anchor, holding in place the doorway between day and night. It is like the *mezuzah*, which we see on our doorways as we exit for our journeys. You can put one on your bedroom door to remind you of the night passage as well. Just as the *mezuzah* reminds us of the first Passover, when the Israelites were protected from destruction in Egypt, so the *Hashkivenu* is also a protection. Moreover, it substitutes for the traditional four-cornered garment with fringes (*tzitzit*). That garment is compared to Divine wings of protection, and the *Hashkivenu* asks God to "shelter us in the shadow of your wings." [5]

Thus, the *Hashkivenu* keeps us connected to the world here below, while at the same time, we connect to the "upper world" through a prayer invoking angels.

Inviting an Angelic Presence

The emphasis on spiritual protection appears in another prayer included in some versions of the bedtime *Shema*: a prayer for angelic protection. The English text reads: "In the Name of *Adonai*, God of Israel: May Michael be at my right, Gabriel at my left, Uriel before me, and Rafael behind me; and above my head the *Shekhinah* of God." [6] Four angels are mentioned here: Michael, whose name means "who is like God" (in Hebrew, *mi-cha-el*), is a messenger angel; Gabriel (*gevurah-el*), the "power of God," protects the good and destroys the wicked; Uriel (*ori-el*), "my light of God," is an angel of light and lights the way in front of us; Rafael (*refuah-el*), "the healing of God," brings health and cures the sick. The fifth presence in the prayer is the *Shekhinah*, the Divine Presence of God in the feminine form. The *Shekhinah* is with us always to provide overarching protection.

Many people do not realize that Judaism incorporates belief in angels. Angels are rarely mentioned in ethical and legal discourse, yet are readily acknowledged in mystical literature. They also appear prominently in our prayers. In the traditional Shabbat service, for instance, the beginning of the *Kedushah* reads as follows:

> We shall sanctify Your Name in this world, just as they [the angels] sanctify it in heaven above, as it is written by your prophet:
> "And one will call another and say, 'Holy, holy, holy is *Adonai* of hosts! The whole world is filled with his Glory." Then, with a sound of great noise, mighty and powerful, they make heard a voice, raising themselves toward the *Seraphim* (fiery angelic beings). Those facing them say 'Blessed: Blessed is the Glory of *Adonai* from his place.'" [7]

Also, the first blessing before the *Shema* refers to "ministering angels" who are "all beloved, all flawless, all mighty, they all do the Will of their Maker with dread and reverence."

Where do all these beings come from? What are they? We tend to think of angels as the chubby little people with wings who appear in Renaissance paintings. But the Bible tells a quite different story. Sometimes angelic beings take on human form. Humanoid angels appear in the story of Abraham feeding the "guests" who appeared suddenly on the road on a hot day. As the commentaries explain, they were angels and each had a distinct mission—one to heal Abraham from his recent circumcision, one to prophesy Isaac's birth for Abraham and Sarah, and one to oversee the destruction of Sodom (Genesis 18–19). Another angel was stationed at the door of the Garden of Eden after the exile of Adam and Eve so they could not reenter (Genesis 3:24). Still another appeared to stop Balaam, a non-Jewish prophet, from continuing on his journey to help defeat the Jewish people (Numbers 22:22–35).

On the other hand, some prophets saw angels quite differently. For instance, Ezekiel, in his famous Vision of the Chariot, saw *Ofanim*, which means "wheels." But these wheel-shaped creatures were living beings who had eyes around their circumference. Ezekiel also saw *Chayot,* which usually means "wild beasts," but in his vision were figures with animal faces. Isaiah, an earlier prophet, saw *Seraphim*, whose name suggests a very intense fire.

The mystics concluded that angels are beings whose primary domain lies in what Jewish mysticism calls the world of formation (*Yetzirah*), a world where pure energies reign. These energies are analogous to the currents of energy that we associate with feelings and emotions. Angels function there much as we function in the world of action (*Asiyah*), fulfilling the inclinations of that world in a way that we might describe as following an inspiration.[8] Angels also transmit vital energy from one world to another, carrying God's messages to us and our messages to God. An angel is conscious and aware, but without the complexity of the human soul. It is one-dimensional and without free choice; it can only carry out the one mission to which it is assigned. That one mission could be delivering a message, singing God's praises, or dispensing death, but each angel has only one kind of act in its repertoire.

Rabbi Adin Steinsaltz, a modern Talmud scholar, explains that some angels have existed forever and are the "channels of plenty" through which Divine grace rises and descends. Perhaps these are the angels Jacob saw in his dream, ascending and descending from one world to the next. Other angels are constantly being created, and some are created from our own thoughts and actions. When we focus on doing a good deed or performing one of the Torah's commandments, for example, our very intent creates an angel.[9]

In this context, we can understand the "spirit of impurity" mentioned earlier, which can affect us even after we are asleep. Steinsaltz calls such influences "subversive angels" because they have been created by acts or thoughts of malice or evil. But he also points out that angels in the realm of evil are like parasites because they depend on human actions for their sustenance. If we refuse to nourish them, they will disappear.[10] When we think of angels of goodness, we turn away from the negative and toward the positive.

The angels of the Bedtime Prayers—Michael, Gabriel, Uriel, and Rafael—have been encountered and recognized through the energy they carry. Their energy-essences (communication, power, light, healing) have been recognized by people at various places and times. Their association with specific energies or powers may remind us of pagan deities, who were frequently connected to the powers of nature, or had certain functions, like bearing messages. This makes some people uncomfortable with the idea of angels. But it is important to remember that Judaism never denied that nature had powers of its own. The powers were real, but the prophets fought against the belief that those powers paralleled God's in any way. God stood far above the powers represented by the deities; their task was to carry out God's Will.

In order that no one will be confused about whether we are praying to lesser powers, the Bedtime Prayers are clear that we are praying in the name of God to ask the angels to protect us. We are not praying to the angels themselves. (Some people may not be comfortable with verbally invoking angels, so we make this optional in the practice of the prayers described at the end of this chapter.) The prayer itself concludes with a request for the presence of the *Shekhinah*. The *Shekhinah*, of course, is always present. The prayer affirms God's embracing presence at this special and intimate time, as we prepare for sleep.

Creating a *Sukkah* of Peace

The *sukkah* is one of the *Hashkivenu*'s most powerful symbols. This is the temporary structure covered with branches that Jews erect each year for the holiday of Sukkot so they can fulfill the Torah's command to live in it for seven days. The *sukkah* (usually translated as "booth" or "hut") symbolizes how God protected the Israelites for the forty years in the desert when they only had temporary housing. Despite the physical fragility of the *sukkah*, it represents a higher level of protection and reminds us that houses of wood and stone are only physical, but Divine protection is the true shelter.

The *sukkah* is also compared to the "clouds of glory" that, according to a midrash, surrounded the Israelites while they were traveling in the desert. The clouds hid the Jewish people from their enemies. Similarly, the *sukkah* and the angelic presences encircle us with protection.

The *sukkah* also represents peace. The Hebrew word for "peace," *shalom*, is related to *shalem*, which means "completion." As the holiday of Sukkot marks the completion of the great cycle of the fall holidays, imagining the *sukkah* of peace brings our day to a close and affirms its completion.

Movement and Meditation for the *Hashkivenu*

Remember that the first of the Bedtime Prayers weaves the energies of protection around us. It asks for specific protection against physical or spiritual dangers, and aids us in visualizing the *sukkah*, the presence of angels, and the *Shekhinah*. (If the images of a *sukkah* and angels do not work for you, visualize a place of complete safety and beauty, with loving presences surrounding you.)

We recommend doing these prayers with movements that involve the whole body. This will deepen your sense of being protected.

Take a moment to become aware of the physical space around you. If possible, touch the *mezuzah* of the room you are in. (Traditionally, you touch it with your fingers, then kiss them lightly). Where you sleep has the potential to be a *makom* where you could say, as Jacob did, "This is none other than a house of God. This is a gate of heaven."

Now imagine the Divine Presence filling your room.

Make sure your bed is made comfortably. As you prepare it (and as you make it the next morning), focus on your intent to be spiritually conscious when you lie down.

Then state your intent. You might say: "I intend to sleep in a calm and peaceful way, like a child of God." Or, "I am preparing for sleep, so that I can strengthen my body for spiritual service, and refresh my mind with positive thoughts and good dreams."[11] Keep it simple, and use words that reflect your own true intent.

Here is the full Hebrew version of the *Hashkivenu* and Invocation of Angels, with English translation:

☐ *Hashkivenu*

הַשְׁכִּיבֵנוּ יהוה אֱלֹהֵינוּ לְשָׁלוֹם,

וְהַעֲמִידֵנוּ מַלְכֵּנוּ לְחַיִּים.

וּפְרוֹשׂ עָלֵינוּ סֻכַּת שְׁלוֹמֶךָ.

וְתַקְּנֵנוּ בְּעֵצָה טוֹבָה מִלְּפָנֶיךָ.

וְהוֹשִׁיעֵנוּ לְמַעַן שְׁמֶךָ. וְהָגֵן בַּעֲדֵנוּ,

וְהָסֵר מֵעָלֵינוּ

אוֹיֵב דֶּבֶר וְחֶרֶב וְרָעָב וְיָגוֹן.

וְהָסֵר שָׂטָן מִלְּפָנֵינוּ וּמֵאַחֲרֵינוּ.

וּבְצֵל כְּנָפֶיךָ תַּסְתִּירֵנוּ.

כִּי אֵל שׁוֹמְרֵנוּ וּמַצִּילֵנוּ אַתָּה,

כִּי אֵל מֶלֶךְ חַנּוּן וְרַחוּם אָתָּה.

וּשְׁמוֹר צֵאתֵנוּ וּבוֹאֵנוּ לְחַיִּים וּלְשָׁלוֹם,

מֵעַתָּה וְעַד עוֹלָם.

Hashkivenu, Adonai Elohenu, leshalom,
veha'amidenu Malkenu lechayim.
Uferos alenu sukkat shelomecha,
vetakenenu b'etzah tovah milfanecha.
Vehoshi'enu lema'an shemecha, vehagen ba'adenu
vehaser me'alenu oyev, dever,
vecherev vera'av veyagon.
Vehaser satan milfanenu ume'acharenu,
uvetzel kenafecha tastirenu.

Ki El shomerenu umatzilenu ata,
ki El Melech chanun verachum ata.
Ushemor tzetenu uvo'enu lechayim uleshalom
me'ata ve'ad olam.

Lay us down, Adonai our God, in peace,
and raise us up, our Ruler, to life.
Spread over us a sukkah of Your peace
and set us right with good counsel from You.
Save us for the sake of Your Name,
shield us and remove from us
enemies, plague, sword, famine, and woe.
And remove spiritual impediment
from before us and behind us,
and shelter us in the shadow of Your wings.
For You are God who protects and rescues us,
for You are God, the gracious and compassionate Ruler.
Safeguard our going and our coming, for life and peace,
now and forever.

☐ Invocation of Angels

בְּשֵׁם יהוה אֱלֹהֵי יִשְׂרָאֵל

וּמִשְׂמֹאלִי גַּבְרִיאֵל מִימִינִי מִיכָאֵל

וּמִלְפָנַי אוּרִיאֵל

וּמֵאֲחוֹרַי רְפָאֵל

וְעַל רֹאשִׁי שְׁכִינַת אֵל

Beshem Adonai Elohei Yisrael
mimeni Michael   umismoli Gavriel
umilfanai Uriel
ume'achorai Refael
v'al roshi Shekhinat El

In the Name of Adonai God of Israel:
May Michael be at my right,   Gabriel at my left,
Uriel before me,
and Rafael behind me;
and above my head the Shekhinah of God.

Following is a shortened version of the *Hashkivenu*, combining Hebrew and English, to use with movements to help you create your *sukkah* of peace as a sacred space for sleep. The words are as follows:

> *Hashkivenu, Adonai Elohenu, leshalom,*
> *veha'amidenu Malkenu lechayim.*
> *Uferos alenu sukkat shelomecha,*
> *vetakenenu b'etzah tova milefanecha.*

> Spread your wings over us and shelter us,
> our God of grace and love.
> Guard us and guide us in our coming
> and going, now and forever.
> Amen. Amen. Amen. Amen. Amen.

Hashkivenu, Adonai Elohenu, leshalom …

1. As you stand, place your hands together above your head with your arms extended (straight elbows).

Lower them down and out and to the sides, making a large upside-down "V."

Veha'amidenu, Malkenu, lechayim.

2. With your arms still down, put your hands together in front of your abdomen,

then bring them up and out to both sides, making a right-side up "V". You have just created a Magen David (six-pointed Jewish star).

Uferos alenu sukkat shelomecha,

3. With your hands still up and out to the sides, rotate your body to the left and the right, so that your hands "draw" a roof over your head.

… uve'etzah tovah takenenu.

4. Slowly bring your hands down to your sides.

Spread your wings over us and shelter us …

5. Incline your head slightly forward. Bring your right hand up and forward from your side in a large arc,

ending with your hand just in front of your head. This creates a "wing" on the right.

6. Repeat the same movement on your left.

Our God of grace and love.

7. Turn your palms upward and raise your head, opening the palms in prayer.

Guard us and guide us in our coming and going, now and forever.

8. Bring your hands down to your heart and then to your sides, palms down.

Amen. Amen. Amen. Amen. Amen. (Chanted very slowly).

9. On each of these "Amens" you will create a counterclockwise circle by turning toward each quadrant. Begin by stepping to your left with your left foot. You will be facing the left quadrant to invoke the angelic energies of that direction. In a welcoming gesture, raise your arms in front of you with palms up, reaching out and up and, in a large swooping motion, bringing the energy in toward yourself as if it were washing over your head, face and body. You may wish to think of Gabriel, the angel of strength and protection.

Step again to the left and repeat the motions. You will now be 180 degrees from your starting position. Imagine that Rafael, the angel of healing, is behind you.

Step again to the left and repeat the motions. Imagine Michael, the messenger angel, on your right.

Step again to the left and repeat. You will now be in your starting position. Think of Uriel, the angel of light, in front of you.

On the last "Amen," turn your head slightly upward and imagine the Divine Presence above your head and extending around you.

10. Relax your arms and head. Stand for a minute or two in silent meditation. Feel the angelic energies around you, guarding your *sukkah* of peace.

רִבּוֹנוֹ שֶׁל עוֹלָם,

הֲרֵינִי מוֹחֵל/מוֹחֶלֶת

לְכָל מִי שֶׁהִכְעִיס וְהִקְנִיט אוֹתִי,

אוֹ שֶׁחָטָא כְּנֶגְדִּי —

בֵּין בְּגוּפִי, בֵּין בְּמָמוֹנִי,

בֵּין בִּכְבוֹדִי,

בֵּין בְּכָל אֲשֶׁר לִי;

בֵּין בְּאוֹנֶס, בֵּין בְּרָצוֹן, בֵּין בְּשׁוֹגֵג, בֵּין בְּמֵזִיד;

בֵּין בְּדִבּוּר בֵּין בְּמַעֲשֶׂה,

בֵּין בְּמַחֲשָׁבָה, בֵּין בְּהִרְהוּר;

בֵּין בְּגִלְגּוּל זֶה, בֵּין בְּגִלְגּוּל אַחֵר —

לְכָל בַּר יִשְׂרָאֵל, וְלֹא יֵעָנֵשׁ שׁוּם אָדָם בְּסִבָּתִי.

יְהִי רָצוֹן מִלְּפָנֶיךָ יהוה אֱלֹהַי וֵאלֹהֵי אֲבוֹתַי,

שֶׁלֹּא אֶחֱטָא עוֹד.

וּמַה שֶּׁחָטָאתִי לְפָנֶיךָ

מְחוֹק בְּרַחֲמֶיךָ הָרַבִּים,

אֲבָל לֹא עַל יְדֵי יִסּוּרִים וַחֲלָיִים רָעִים.

יִהְיוּ לְרָצוֹן אִמְרֵי פִי וְהֶגְיוֹן לִבִּי לְפָנֶיךָ,

יהוה צוּרִי וְגֹאֲלִי.

Master of the universe,
I hereby forgive everyone who angered
or antagonized me, or sinned against me—
whether against my body or my property,
my honor or anything of mine,
whether accidentally or willfully, carelessly or purposely,
whether by speech or deed, thought or fantasy,
whether in this incarnation or in another incarnation,
—may no one be punished because of me.

May it be your will, Adonai my God and God of my ancestors,
that I may sin no more.
Whatever my error before You,
may it be blotted out in Your abundant mercies,
but not through suffering or severe illness.
May the expressions of my mouth
and the thoughts of my heart be pleasing to you,
Adonai, my Rock and my Redeemer.

im until

He said, "Not Jacob shall your name be spoken any more, but Israel, for you have striven with God and with men, and have prevailed."

—Genesis 32:25–29

Joseph dreamed another dream and related it to his brothers. And he said, "Look, I dreamed another dream: Behold! The sun, the moon, and eleven stars were bowing down to me...."

When Joseph came to the house they brought the tribute that was in their hands to him at the house, and they prostrated themselves to him toward the ground....

> Then Joseph said to his brothers, "Come close to me, if you
> please," and they came close. And he said, "I am Joseph your
> brother—it is I, whom you sold into Egypt. And now, be not
> distressed, nor reproach yourselves for having sold me here, for
> it was to be a provider that God sent me ahead of you .... It was
> not you who sent me here but God."
>
> —Genesis 37:9, 43:26, 45:4–8

Two of the great dreamers in the Bible are Jacob and Joseph. Jacob dreamed of things he hardly knew. He dreamed about angels on ladders and about wrestling with an angel—a dream that left a physical trace on his body in the form of a limp. In these dreams, he said that God's house and God's face were revealed to him.

The dreams of Joseph, who was the son of Jacob and Rachel, were prophetic. His early dreams were highly symbolic: His brothers' sheaves of wheat bowed down to his, and the stars and moon bowed down to him. These sowed discord between him and his brothers, but they came true when his brothers kneeled before him after he became Egypt's prime minister. He could interpret other people's dreams so well that he became a diviner in Pharaoh's court.

But neither the spirituality of Jacob's dreams nor the prophetic symbolism of Joseph's will concern us here. Jacob had been in conflict with his twin brother Esau ever since their youth, and Esau's rage had forced him to leave their ancestral home. Joseph was nearly killed by his brothers, and they sold him into slavery. As a result, he had been in exile from his birthplace and separated from his beloved father for more than twenty years. Because both Jacob and Joseph had to come to terms with long, deep enmity in their own families, each of these dreamers gives us a clue to understanding another of the Bedtime Prayers—the Prayer of Forgiveness.[1]

Forgiving, and Pursuing Justice

First, let's look carefully at the wording of the prayer. The Prayer of Forgiveness that appears in our traditional texts is striking because it expresses total and complete forgiveness and absolution:

> I hereby forgive each person who angered or antagonized me,
> or sinned against me—
> whether against my body or my property, my honor or any-
> thing of mine,
> whether accidentally or willfully, unintentionally or purposely,
> whether by speech or deed, thought or fantasy,
> whether in this incarnation or in another incarnation,
> —everyone, and may no one be punished because of me.[2]

On the one hand, the prayer offers a breathtaking spiritual vision. It refers to all aspects of our lives and all aspects of the forgiven person's intention—even if he or she fantasized about doing something to us! In addition, it refers to other lives we have lived, of which we normally have no recollection. On the other hand, the prayer presents a problem. Indeed, it is almost offensive to Jewish concepts of justice: How can you forgive people who have not indicated they are even aware of the sins they committed against you?

Certainly, we are encouraged to be forgiving, and to be generous in our forgiveness, when anyone with even a little contrition approaches us. Every year, every Jew is supposed to ask forgiveness before Yom Kippur from anyone they may have offended, because "Yom Kippur atones for sins between a human being and God, but not between one human being and another." If we ask a person three times to forgive us, and they refuse to do so, the burden of sin then falls on them. In this situation, the person who has erred is the one who must initiate the process of forgiveness. But in the forgiveness prayer, the one who forgives begins the task. This seems an aberration, or at least a puzzle.

There is yet another problem. In anything other than a personal relationship, some atonement or reparation is expected. Talmudic law records lengthy and detailed deliberations over the monetary or other benefits that offenders are required to pay whomever they have harmed. Careful distinctions are made between accidental and intentional injury to determine the exact nature of the crime. But in the forgiveness prayer, even in cases where our property or body has been harmed and we might have a right to seek legal redress, we are pronouncing absolution.

What is behind this prayer is a very radical notion: We must forgive. Unless we do, we torment ourselves. Forgiveness can be very difficult, but we can do it if we want to. We have to want peace more than anything else. And this peace is for ourselves, so that we no longer torment our minds with old stories, our hearts with resentment, or our bodies with the stress of inner struggle.

Simon Weisenthal brought this issue of forgiveness to the fore in his book, *The Sunflower*. Weisenthal, a Holocaust survivor, is known throughout the world for finding ex-Nazis and bringing them to trial. In *The Sunflower*, he tells about a dying German SS soldier who told him the story of his life—essentially a deathbed confession—and asked Weisenthal's forgiveness for his killing of Jews. Weisenthal listened to the story, then turned away without saying a word. Still, the incident remained with him, and he questioned whether he had done the right thing by not forgiving the soldier. Eventually he wrote about the incident, then sent the manuscript to a variety of people—religious thinkers and literary figures, Jews and non-Jews, Holocaust survivors and others who had not been through the horrors of those times. He asked each to write a short piece discussing whether they thought he had made the right decision to leave without forgiving the soldier.[3]

Interestingly, almost all the Jewish respondents supported Weisenthal's refusal to forgive the Nazi soldier. First of all, they pointed out, Weisenthal could not stand in the place of those who had been killed. Only the victims could grant forgiveness. Some suggested that was one reason why murder is an unforgivable crime: The victims cannot confront the murderer and demand amends. The soldier was acting in the belief that one Jew could stand for others, which may have been a tribute to the unity of the people, but also hints of the Christian idea that a person (such as a priest) can stand in God's place to grant forgiveness. Yet, as mentioned earlier, Judaism holds that even God cannot forgive crimes against human beings if the person has not sought forgiveness from the people he hurt.

Then there was the matter of reparations. In the case of murder, this would mean that, according to Torah, the perpetrator could be punished with death. Jewish law preserved leniency in these matters by making the criteria for proving crimes very demanding. A crime had to have two witnesses, and they had to meet many criteria to ensure that they were honest and had not conspired against the accused. Distinctions were made between manslaughter and murder, between premeditated crimes and what would now be called "crimes of passion." As a result, in the days when Jewish courts had the power to decree a death penalty (when

Israel was independent and the Temple still stood), executions were still quite rare. The saying was that a *Sanhedrin* (the Supreme Court) that executed one man in seventy years was considered a harsh court. Still, monetary damages were demanded of anyone who committed a crime against another person, even if it was only by carelessness.

The German soldier was not offering reparations. Did he think his own death at a young age was atonement for his crimes, along with his confession? Even if we can see how he might take that perspective, the whole procedure of justice is undermined if an individual thinks he can determine his own just punishment.

Judaism's traditional emphasis on careful, thoughtful procedures of justice instilled in Jews a sensitivity toward the feelings of the victim as well as the rights of the accused. A criminal could not be punished without a fair trial, in which all factors would be considered by people who could see the matter clearly—an impartial court knowledgeable in Jewish law. If guilt was ascertained, victims had a right to reparations that were proportionate to the pain they had suffered. (The biblical phrase "an eye for an eye, a tooth for a tooth" is, in Judaism, a metaphor for appropriate reparations, not a prescription for revenge.)

Spiritual Dimensions of Forgiveness

Flying in the face of all this comes the bedtime forgiveness prayer, which asserts a general forgiveness to each and all, now and in the unknown past, not only offering forgiveness from the individual but also requesting an amnesty from God: "May no person be punished on my account." How can this be accommodated to the traditional Jewish sense of justice?

First, it is clear that in saying the forgiveness prayer, we are not forgiving on behalf of anyone else. This is a personal prayer, not one of the collective prayers commonly used in Jewish liturgy referring to "us." This removes one objection that was raised in the case of the Nazi soldier, who was asking one Jew to forgive what he had done to many others.

Yet, isn't it appropriate to expect that, before we forgive, the person who has harmed us will ask forgiveness? Normally, yes. This is part of the reciprocity that characterizes human society; it is the only way that justice can be done on this earth. That is why establishing courts of justice is a requirement not only for Jews but for non-Jews; it is one of the seven Noachide commandments. (Rabbinic tradition determined that the Torah contains seven commandments incumbent on all human beings: not to worship any deity except the One God; not to blaspheme, murder, steal, commit adultery, or be cruel to animals; and to set up courts of justice.)

But the situation of the bedtime forgiveness prayer is different. The crux of the matter is that this is not a court; the Bedtime Prayers have nothing to do with human society and its requirements. We are at a doorway, an entry point into another realm. We are preparing to enter into the dream world, where our souls will be traveling in the realm of spirit. We are moving into a realm not circumscribed or defined by ordinary human norms. We are about to make a soul journey.

This explains some bizarre features of the forgiveness prayer. Can you imagine a person asking forgiveness for a fantasy he had about harming you? "The other day I saw your new car and the thought popped into my mind: 'What would it be like to steal that car and drive it around the block?' I'm really sorry I did that to you." You might think that your friend should see a therapist, but you don't expect him to ask your forgiveness for the fantasy. And you don't have to ask him for forgiveness for thinking he should see a therapist.

Human society and human justice deal with actual harm done in the physical realm, or in Kabbalistic terms *Asiyah*, which is the world of action. Such harm may include emotional and mental suffering, but it can be supported by evidence available to anyone. Likewise, atonement and reparations have to be physical, such as money or another benefit that is given to the person who was harmed.

In personal relationships, we come a little closer to the spiritual realities of the forgiveness prayer. When a spouse says something inappropriate to his or her partner, the actual hurt may be so subtle that only the couple themselves would realize an injury had been done. "I'm sorry" may be enough because the two people involved know each other so well that they can intuit the extent of the atonement that is needed. Yet there are good reasons why a bouquet of flowers often accompanies the "I'm sorry" of a husband, or an extra-special dinner comes with the "I'm sorry" of a wife. A sensitive person recognizes an extra measure of physical comfort can help the person who was hurt. That is the way of the world of *Asiyah*.

In the higher worlds, which our souls have access to during sleep, the rules are still more refined. Every thought, every fantasy carries a certain reality. The energy is subtle and complex. We may think of a feather floating in the breeze, affected by every slight movement of air; yet even its slight weight pulls it slowly toward earth. When the soul enters into the dream world, we want it to be as weightless as possible so that it is free to do its work. Every emotion, every attachment to the earthly world, pulls it back toward the sleeping body and the dormant mind. The soul's first commitment is to heal our psyche, and it can spend the whole night doing that. But if we free it from the attachments of earthly life beforehand, from our pain and worldly involvement, the soul can accomplish much more.[4]

A Personal Story about Struggling to Forgive

Perhaps it will be possible to come to a deeper and more personal understanding through a story of how forgiveness can unfold in an individual's life. It is a true story—one of the authors story—about an event in which forgiveness seemed almost impossible:

"I grew up as one of five children in an upper-middle-class family in Ohio. My father was a prominent attorney, my mother a housewife until my siblings and I were teenagers. My mother then went back to school to get a degree in psychology. Both my parents were deeply involved in supporting Jewish causes, the State of Israel, Jewish education, and Jewish identification. We lived in the safety and beauty of a Cleveland suburb.

"My mother and father loved cultural events, and there was nothing unusual about their going out one night in December 1975 with another couple to see a play. After the play, as they were walking to their car, three teenage boys stopped them on the sidewalk and demanded money. One boy had a sawed-off shotgun, and he pointed it nervously at the group. As the men reached for their wallets, the gun suddenly went off. The boy with the gun had panicked. The boys ran and were caught by the police.

"The gun had been pointing at my father. He was killed immediately. My mother had to go home and tell her children the shocking news.

"I was in Canada visiting friends that night. I'll never forget being awakened, far too early in the morning, by my cousin Moe, who gave me the news and drove me to the airport. What I remember most profoundly after that is a sudden shift in my sense of time. Everything seemed to happen in slow motion. I could barely understand what my cousin said to me; I was frozen. Then I felt myself enclosed by a Presence of thick well-being that escorted me from his home onto the airplane. Once in the air, I looked at the beauty of the clouds sparkling in the sun, and I knew that, as great as the pain was, we were all going to be okay. I knew that a Presence was with me now, something I didn't have before. I experienced what could almost be a form of joy for my father and myself. This infused me with strength I didn't know I had; a strength that I felt must have come from some other source.

"As time passed, the reality of brokenness began to gnaw at my family and at me. Family gatherings became painful. I knew that life would never be the same again. I could no longer see the world as a carefree place, and I envied anyone who could.

"Questions consumed my mind. How could God let a wonderful, vibrant Jew come to an end like this? What did a girl of fifteen do to deserve being robbed of a father to share her life with? Why did it have to happen in such a terrible way? How would I ever heal this? Why did our justice system—which my father had worked for—not bring the boys to justice? How can I feel safe knowing that those boys—and others like them—were still on the streets? Many years later, I still found myself asking how I could help my children feel safe, knowing what I knew.

"Later, my mother told me the killer had written her from jail and asked her forgiveness. Could she dare to forgive? It seemed too difficult. My family rarely talks about the event now, but I wonder if my mother still replays in her mind the horrific scene of watching her husband being killed. I know I do.

"I was angry for a long time—at God, at the world, at my pain, and at myself for not being able to forget the pain. I was angry that I didn't have a father. As I grew older, I kept thinking of what my father missed. He never met my husband or my two beautiful children. He never got to see his fifteen grandchildren. He never got to read the books I wrote or watch me sing *Kol Nidrei* on Yom Kippur.

"This was the painful reality, and I couldn't change it. Sometimes I imagine I would have felt better if the boys responsible for the murder had been punished more severely. Because of their youth, they served a few years in a juvenile detention center and then were freed. But even if the punishment had been greater, I might still feel it wasn't enough. The question remained: Could I forgive?

"I had to forgive. That was the only way to heal the anger, sadness, and pain that I had lived with. It is the remedy, or at least the necessary catalyst for healing. In the process, I learned that if there is justice in the world or in the cosmos, forgiveness doesn't have a whole lot to do with it. They are two separate things.

"I continue to work and wrestle, like Jacob, with the angel of forgiveness. I can only pass along the wisdom of experiencing forgiveness, knowing that it is not the cure. I learned that I have to continue living life to the fullest. If I torment myself with questions or thoughts of revenge, I waste my energy. The best thing I can do is let the events of the past be what they were, and give my pain and my heart to God. That has been one of my hardest lessons in life. Another is whether I can trust and have faith in a God who allowed this to happen.

"I have found that God has been in my life to help me cope, in the same way that a Presence surrounded me when tragedy hit. I love the God that has helped me to move on, to sing and learn, to write and to express my Judaism. When I talk about having found the ability to forgive, I am not absolving that boy of his crime. His earthly payment may have been made, and God takes care of true justice. But I have been able to 'for-give'—to give the hateful energy of pain and revenge to God, and I have been released from it, most of the time.

"My father was famous for one saying that encapsulates his belief. He raised his glass of orange juice every morning and called out, 'Here's to love!' My lesson is that healing through unspeakable tragedy is God's love, even though it takes a good deal of work to uncover it.

"So Dad, here's to love!"

Untangling Ourselves from Pain

The pain that others cause us is a real wound. We can't forget it. It is part of what we carry in life. Imagine a tree that has been split by lightning but is not dead. The wound is right at the heart of the tree. Its huge scar is exhibited for all to see. Yet above the scarred trunk, two great branches continue growing, putting forth more branches and leaves, year after year. The wound has healed over, but the life of the tree is certainly not the same as it would have been if lightning had not struck. And somehow, it still keeps growing.

Our biblical text tells a similar story. Let's return to Jacob, wrestling with the mysterious angel all night. Here is the full text of the passage cited at the beginning of this chapter:

> Jacob was left alone; and a man wrestled with him until the break of dawn. When he saw that he could not prevail against him, he touched the hollow of his thigh, and the hollow of Jacob's thigh was strained as he wrestled with him.
> He said, "Let me go, for the dawn is breaking!"
> He said, "I will not let you go unless you bless me."
> He said to him, "What is your name?"
> He said, "Jacob."
> He said, "Not Jacob shall your name be spoken any more, but Israel, for you have striven with God and with men, and have prevailed."
> Jacob asked and said, "Tell me, please, your name."

He said, "Why do you ask my name?" and he blessed him there.

Jacob called the name of the place Peniel, "For I have seen God face to face, and my soul is preserved."

—Genesis 32:25–31

There are several mysterious dimensions to this text. We are not told the identity of the "man" with whom Jacob wrestled, nor does Jacob ever learn it directly. Various commentators see it differently, but many think that Jacob wrestled with the protective angel of Jacob's twin brother, Esau. The text itself deliberately hides and confuses identities, with the repetition of "He said" for both speakers. Ultimately, Jacob receives a new name, and names the place where they wrestled in a way that suggests he had wrestled not with a representative of Esau, but of God.

The rabbis who spoke of the man as Esau's angel follow a line of interpretation that would not be strange to many modern psychological commentators. The day before his nocturnal encounter, Jacob had made preparations to meet Esau, whom he had not seen for twenty years and then under difficult circumstances—he had deceived their father into giving him his brother's blessing. Esau, as a result, was in a rage. Jacob had been preparing to give Esau large gifts to appease him; if necessary he was ready for war. The appearance of Esau's angel in these circumstances could be ascribed to Jacob's anxiety.

But we would be missing the deeper dimensions of this encounter if we saw it simply as an outgrowth of the unresolved conflict between two brothers. The angel who is "he," who is "the Divine Face," is also Jacob's inner-wrestling. Jacob had put the conflict with Esau behind him for twenty years as he made a fortune and raised a family. Now, returning to his homeland, he had to confront the debris of the life he left behind—including what he did to his twin brother.

Wrestling represents an encounter between two entities that are entangled. In this match, neither party wins. They continue to be entwined until the angel demands, "Let me go, for the dawn is breaking!" Only by letting go can Jacob achieve a new level of integration, which is represented by his new name *Isra-El*, the Wrestler of God.

The night of the wrestling represents the time of Jacob's exile; the daybreak, his return home. During that whole twenty years of his exile, inwardly he had been tied up with his brother in fear and guilt; now he was being told to let go. Jacob, whose name alludes to the deception he performed at his mother's bidding, had to give up that identity so that he could fulfill his destiny, to prevail with God and with human beings.

But would Esau forgive him? Jacob doubted it, so he prayed and sent Esau gifts and prepared for war. The dream, however, reassured him that even if Esau was not ready to forgive, Jacob could release the bonds that held him and move on. We may imagine that Jacob carried his own resentments of Esau, who had been so favored by their father Isaac. These, too, he had to let go.

The next day, the two met. Esau fell weeping on his brother's neck. The twins, who had gone on such separate paths, were reunited. Yet some traditional commentators are not sanguine about this reunion. The story hints that Esau would have preferred to take his brother under armed guard to his own territory. A midrash tells us that when Esau fell on Jacob's neck, he tried to bite him. Perhaps this story suggests that Esau may not have been so willing to let go of his pain, to disentangle. He may have continued to dwell on the wounds of the past.

Whether the forgiveness and the letting go were mutual is not the point. Jacob-Israel is our model here. He was able to disengage from the past and renew his life, even to go back to his old territory and complete his work, but now with a new identity, a new and separate sense of self. Like the lightning-struck tree, he carried an emblem of his struggle—a limp because the angel had injured him in the thigh while they wrestled. But he went on to establish his family in the land that would be named after him and his wrestling.

This is what the forgiveness prayer asks us to do: to disengage, disentangle. We are elevating the mind and heart out of the snarls of our emotions. This process is the vehicle by which we move, level by level, to a sacred path of life. If you feel hesitant to forgive, remember the cost you are paying for resentment and anger—costs to your body in terms of physical energy and health, costs to your clarity of mind and purpose. Collectively also, we can no longer afford the self-centered luxury of each person waiting for someone else to make the move. We must forgive others and ask that we be forgiven.

The steps we can take are clear:

☐ Acknowledge fully the entanglement, the "wrestling" with the people in your lives, and the feelings associated with those relationships. Whenever there is an emotional charge in a relationship, we are in a wrestling match. Analyze and name the feelings, and own them as yours.

☐ Admit your part in creating the entanglements. "What is your name?" "Jacob"—which can mean the "deceiver." Here you may find helpful the traditional process known as *vidui*, or confession, as taught by Maimonides: Admit what you did wrong. Feel remorse. Resolve not to do it again.

☐ Make a leap of faith. Believe that you don't have to be trapped by those feelings, that you can prevail and assert yourself in relation to your higher soul, just as Jacob was renamed Israel.

☐ Give thanks to God that you have had these lessons and experiences in order to refine yourself: "He named the place Peniel" for his "soul was preserved."

☐ Let go. Walk away from the entanglements and toward the possibilities of new relationships. Whether the other person is ready to do this is not your business. Just as Jacob left and went on his journey, so must each of us.

At the end of this chapter, you will find meditative exercises that we have found extremely helpful to go through this process. In addition, writing your story or sharing it with a trusted friend may aid you in your own forgiveness work.

Compassion Brings Us Freedom

In short, the forgiveness prayer asks us to work through our own personal emotional attachments to the pain we have suffered and the people who have brought us suffering. We do this by forgiving from the deepest part of ourselves.

Does this mean that people who did wrong cannot be brought to justice or be asked to make amends for their behavior? Not at all. We have a responsibility to continue to bring justice into the world whenever possible. However, if we free ourselves from our attachment to the suffering we experienced, we can actually bring individuals to justice with a clearer mind and heart. Free of desire for revenge, we can make sure the punishment really fits the crime and that we are not asking for amends only for personal satisfaction. We make amends because that is what we need to do to correct the social and cosmic balance, to rebalance the scales of good and evil in our lives. Our job is not to satisfy others' emotional needs. In a way, that is what happened with Simon Weisenthal's life work: To right the cosmic balance, not from desire for revenge but from a clear heart, with knowledge of doing God's work in the human world.

But what of asking for God's absolution? "May no person be punished because of me." Again, we can make the distinction between the earthly and the heavenly courts, as it were. On earth, we receive the consequences of our behavior. From the perspective of the "heavenly court," however, we have to look at things differently. We have to understand the Jewish concept of punishment by God, whether in this life or in the next.

Most probably, "may no person be punished on my account" refers to life after death. When a person dies and the soul is called up to review its life on earth, the soul will see everything it has done. It's as if the soul has its own personal video of its earthly life, including every significant action—good or evil. In the traditional Jewish metaphor, angels for the defense and angels for the prosecution will line up on either side. This means that the spiritual result of every action will become absolutely clear to the soul, and it will begin its process of refinement or purgation (traditionally, *Gehinnom*), which involves the emotional attachments, or *ruach* level of the soul.[5]

When we ask that a person not be punished on that level, we say, in effect, that we don't want our earthly suffering to make it any harder for another soul. We can imagine our higher self saying, "I want to be on the side of compassion. I know that whatever this person did to me helped me learn and grow, even though it was painful. When they see me in their life's video, let them not see the pain so much as the truth that came out of it." We are asking for an emotional disentangling so that higher knowledge can be experienced.

Is there Divine justice in this life? Judaism answers this question in different ways. One is the idea of *midah k'neged midah*, "measure for measure." The way a person acts will be mirrored in the way others act toward him. For example, Jacob deceived Esau into giving him the birthright; later Jacob was deceived by Laban, who gave him Leah instead of Rachel as his first wife. Another kind of Divine punishment mentioned in Scripture is being "cut off," which some interpret as being spiritually separated from God, while others interpret in terms of sufferings from natural phenomena, such as illness or natural disasters, or early death.

In either case, we cannot judge. The ethical teachers of Judaism emphasize over and over again that we do not have God's perspective. Each person is judged according to his or her own ability and level of moral decision-making. This is called the *bechirah*-point, the point of free will. For example, a person who grows up in an environment where thievery is a way of life may not even consider that stealing is wrong. However, he may eventually have to consider whether he should shoot a person so he can steal something. He may not truly have free choice about stealing because he has never considered the question or been taught differently, but free choice enters when he decides whether to pull the trigger. On the other hand, someone who is raised in a refined, moral environment may struggle with whether to gossip about someone, and that is his point of free choice.[6]

As we grow spiritually and morally, our individual *bechirah*-point changes. At one point, a person may take it for granted that he can cheat on his taxes; a few years later, he no longer cheats on taxes, but has to fight with himself about how much to give to charity.

When we think about this, we realize that we can never know what blame or praise to place on another person's actions. The people who have hurt you may not have been sufficiently in control of themselves to have intentionally done anything wrong, so how could they need forgiveness if they were in the grip of forces beyond their control?

Ultimately, this leads us to a more complete fulfillment of two very precious *mitzvot*: "Do not hate your brother in your heart," and "Do not take revenge." When we can stop holding grudges, when we can trust the operations of justice in God's world and work toward justice in our own, we move into a stronger, clearer, more compassionate mode of being.

When we can be more forgiving of others, we can ask for forgiveness, as the prayer continues: "Whatever my error before you, may it be blotted out in your abundant mercies." A story is told that on a certain Yom Kippur, Abraham Isaac Kook, the chief Ashkenazic rabbi of Palestine until his death in 1935, was especially joyful. When a friend asked why, he replied that before Yom Kippur he had been careful to forgive everyone, even those who had not asked his forgiveness. Then he realized, during the Yom Kippur prayers, that even if he forgot something he was supposed to ask God for forgiveness for, God would probably forgive him anyway, because he had tried to be so complete in his own forgiveness.[7]

In this way, we can be compassionate to ourselves, recognizing that sometimes we make bad choices, whether from ignorance or pure egotism. The important thing is that once we see this, we are already moving to a different point of choice.

In fact, this is the most important and clearest result of the forgiveness prayer: what happens to the person who does the forgiving. When we allow God to take care of Divine business, we lighten our own burdens. Forgiving means "for-giving," giving it to God. What we cannot expect (though sometimes it happens unexpectedly) is that the person who offended us will change. That also has to be left to God.

Seeing the Grand Design

Now we can turn to the other story of a dreamer—Joseph, the favorite son of Jacob. As a youth, Joseph dreamed that his brothers and his father would bow down to him. The brothers, seeing him as dangerously arrogant, sold him into slavery. Through his divinatory powers, Joseph rose to high position. In the twists and turns of the story, the brothers, seeking relief from the famine that was sweeping the land of Israel, ended up coming to Egypt and, literally, bowed down to Joseph.

Joseph actually worked on earthly and spiritual planes simultaneously. Because of his position in Egypt, he turned out to be the appointed agent to deal with his brothers' sins against him. He put them through a long process of questioning and self-examination to make sure their repentance was complete for what they had done to him. He sent them back to Canaan, insisting that they bring his brother Benjamin with them so that he could see whether they would betray another brother as they had betrayed him. Thus he could precisely test their moral fiber—their *teshuvah*, or repentance.

Joseph could do this because he was not seeking revenge. He demonstrated throughout his own trials that he was placing his faith in God, and he clearly believed that God was the guiding hand in the string of events that had led to the family's reunion. Long before his brothers arrived in Egypt, he had forgiven them. Thus he could set up the conditions for their test of *teshuvah* without being invested in the result. He could give them a teaching that would purify the relationships within the family. Because he worked from a place of forgiveness, he could also wholeheartedly seek reconciliation. "Come close to me," he begged his brothers. "Be not distressed, nor reproach yourselves…. It was not you who sent me here but God."

Joseph successfully forgave because he could see the larger picture. In the process of forgiveness—and it is a process, not a one-time action—we change our own perspective on the hurt we have suffered. We allow pain to become a lesson instead of a constant torment. This means trusting that the circumstances that brought pain were ultimately from God, and that we became enmeshed in them because we needed to learn the lesson. Sometimes our lessons are quick and easy, even though painful, like a child learning not to touch a hot stove. Sometimes they are long and difficult, and we do not really see what we learned until many years after, as with a person who suffers years of abuse. In the final analysis, it is only possible to forgive the perpetrator completely if we understand that the pain of life, as well as its good moments, are all part of a grand design to release our full potential as spiritual beings.

In many cases, however, that is not so easy—neither the understanding nor the forgiveness. But both can be done if we commit ourselves to doing this work each day. We have seen it happen in many forms among people of vastly different temperaments. The main thing is to make it part of a regular practice, to develop the capacities of forgiveness and faith just as we develop our physical muscles and mental abilities. The meditations that follow can be used as part of the Bedtime Prayers ritual to help you learn, little by little, how to release pain, to be grateful for whatever lessons you have received, and to give the ultimate outcome—whatever that may be—over to God.

The Forgiveness Prayer with Meditations

We highly recommend doing a forgiveness meditation frequently, concluding with a reading of the traditional forgiveness prayer, or whatever portions of it you find comfortable. Recognize that as you prepare to say the prayer, you may not be willing to grant complete forgiveness to even one person. You may instead prefer to say to God, "I am reading this prayer even though I cannot yet do what it says. Help me be willing to forgive more and more."

We suggest that you start with one person who has affronted you in a minor way so you can become accustomed to the dynamic of forgiving. Often it's too difficult to start by trying to forgive an abusive parent or a person you face in your life every day. Perhaps you will start with an accidental insult from a co-worker or with the fifth-grade teacher who embarrassed you many years ago. Take one person, one incident at a time. Eventually you may recapitulate your whole life in this way. You will even come to a point where you want to clear yourself of apparently positive attachments that no longer serve your spiritual growth. But begin with the small things, learn from each one, and move on to more difficult ones gradually. When you find that you cannot forgive a certain person, again ask God to help you be willing to forgive in the future. Put that incident or relationship aside and continue with others, returning to the more difficult ones at a later time.

We also include here two other meditations: one for forgiving yourself, and one asking for another person's forgiveness. Of course, you can adapt the meditation and visualization to your own needs, using different images or words, after you become familiar with the process. The most important thing is to do the exercise—and do it regularly.

1. Forgiving Another Person

Close your eyes and breathe deeply, in and out. Let your body settle into your chair or bed. Become aware of your physical body and how you are sitting or lying. What is the temperature of your body? What is the taste in your mouth? Is there fear or tension in your body? Gently tell your body that it is okay to relax now because you have finished your day. Give thanks to God for helping you complete a day to the best of your ability.

Now close your eyes. You are ready to open your inner eyes and experience a place where you have the gift of inner vision. As you inwardly imagine yourself in your sukkah *of peace, notice that on one side of it the curtains part, and you see before you a magnificently moonlit beach. See yourself stepping out of the* sukkah *onto a path made of natural stones, which is also lit by the moon. As you place your feet on the smooth stones, the light glistens and illuminates your feet as well. You become aware of a warm blanket being placed around your shoulders to protect and comfort you. You can hear the sound of the ocean as you approach. The air is fresh and cool against your nostrils.*

Breathe in and breathe out. Open your arms wide like a bird. The breeze blows right through you, cleansing away any tension or residue from the day. It takes away any impurities, blocks, or resistance from your inner being. They seem to dissolve into the air.

A sense of freedom and expansiveness fills you. Notice whether there are any places where the wind, the ruach, *cannot blow freely. Gently focus on that area and send the breeze lovingly to that place. Notice what the breeze feels like as it blows through your mind and senses ... your throat, your heart ... your solar plexus, your belly, hips, pelvis, groin. It blows through your spine and the muscles of your back, arms, and legs. You become a hollow reed as it moves freely through you.*

If you are ready, it is now time to do some forgiveness work. Ask yourself: Am I ready to let go and untie myself from what does not serve my soul's mission in this world? From relationships and experiences that drain my energy? If the answer is yes, you are ready to "for-give" this to God so you can learn, release, and move forward in wisdom.

Begin to notice the beauty of the vast dark ocean before you. The moonlight begins to shine on the waves in a way that brings up pictures of the day's events—people you encountered, business you were involved in, everyday tasks. The scenes may shift to the past week or to events from the past year. Trust whatever presents itself. Perhaps nothing will appear, and that is fine, too. Just keep making the space for whatever or whoever needs to appear. Ask God to help you be willing to face and heal the feelings inside you.

Whoever appears before you will be the one from whose painful acts, betrayal, or abandonment you need to be healed. It doesn't matter if this is a highly significant person in your life, or someone you met only once in the grocery store. The important thing is that the encounter left you with a certain emotional resonance.

When the person's image becomes clear enough for you to recognize, thank the person for coming. Try not to judge what you are feeling about the person. Simply allow the painful feeling to arise.

Imagine that a strand of light extends from your heart or solar plexus to the same area on the other person's body. This strand may be as thick as a rope or as thin as a thread. It represents the energy that attaches you to this person. Feel the energy of the event that caused you pain. Do not judge it. Just feel it. This is energy that is being taken from your body and psyche to sustain your attachment to this event with this person. What does it feel like? Is it leaking out in dribbles, or pouring out like a flood of tears? Is it blocked?

Try to name the feeling of your pain. Describe your perception of it. Tell the person before you about your feelings, remembering to stay with your feelings. Avoid getting involved in talking about their feelings, remembered or imagined. For example, "I feel angry that you walked out of my life and started a new one." "I feel betrayed that you spend time on your work instead of with me." "I feel resentful that you did not protect me." Keep the feelings in the present tense. Be clear about the event or experience. How did it harm you? Did it harm your body, your property, your honor, or your self-esteem? Did the injury come through your friends or family? Was it done accidentally or willfully? Through speech or through an action? Did it occur in this incarnation or perhaps in another?

Once you have stated the feelings, try to see whether there was a lesson to learn, a life experience you needed to face and master through your encounter with this person. Now that you have named it and seen it clearly, you are ready to let go. You have the choice to stop carrying this burden.

Now we are ready for giving this experience to God, Ruler of all souls, to judge and heal.

Keep breathing. Look at this person and thank them for the experience they brought into your life. Tell them that you have learned your life lesson and that you are ready to move on now. Thank God for the lesson and for Divine help to move on. Take a long deep breath and slowly exhale it.

Look again at the strand of light that connects you to this person. Notice that midway along it there is a bow that ties the strands together. Reach out with your right hand and pull on the strand that releases the bow, untying the knot.

The strand of light will now spiral back counterclockwise into the center of your own body. It warms, soothes, and relaxes the muscles of your stomach. As you breathe, the relaxation moves into your chest, relaxing the muscles around your heart and lungs. The warmth and light and relaxation now spread into your arms and legs, hands and feet, then into your face, relaxing the muscles around your mouth and eyes. With it comes confidence and strength.

You are free. You have let go. You may notice that the image of the person before you has changed, softened, or even faded. The other person is now free to do his or her own work with God.

Now say the Prayer of Forgiveness.

רִבּוֹנוֹ שֶׁל עוֹלָם,

הֲרֵינִי מוֹחֵל/מוֹחֶלֶת

לְכָל מִי שֶׁהִכְעִיס וְהִקְנִיט אוֹתִי,

אוֹ שֶׁחָטָא כְּנֶגְדִּי —

בֵּין בְּגוּפִי, בֵּין בְּמָמוֹנִי,

בֵּין בִּכְבוֹדִי,

בֵּין בְּכָל אֲשֶׁר לִי;

בֵּין בְּאוֹנֶס, בֵּין בְּרָצוֹן, בֵּין בְּשׁוֹגֵג, בֵּין בְּמֵזִיד;

בֵּין בְּדִבּוּר בֵּין בְּמַעֲשֶׂה,

בֵּין בְּמַחֲשָׁבָה, בֵּין בְּהִרְהוּר;

בֵּין בְּגִלְגּוּל זֶה, בֵּין בְּגִלְגּוּל אַחֵר —

לְכָל בַּר יִשְׂרָאֵל, וְלֹא יֵעָנֵשׁ שׁוּם אָדָם בְּסִבָּתִי.

יְהִי רָצוֹן מִלְּפָנֶיךָ יהוה אֱלֹהַי וֵאלֹהֵי אֲבוֹתַי,

שֶׁלֹּא אֶחֱטָא עוֹד.

וּמַה שֶׁחָטָאתִי לְפָנֶיךָ

מְחוֹק בְּרַחֲמֶיךָ הָרַבִּים,

אֲבָל לֹא עַל יְדֵי יִסּוֹרִים וָחֳלָיִים רָעִים.

יִהְיוּ לְרָצוֹן אִמְרֵי פִי וְהֶגְיוֹן לִבִּי לְפָנֶיךָ,

יהוה צוּרִי וְגוֹאֲלִי.

Ribono shel olam,
Hareni mochel/mochelet
lechol mi shehichis vehiknit oti,
o shechata kenegdi—
bein begufi, bein bemamoni,
bein bichvodi, bein bechol asher li,
bein be'ones, bein beratzon, bein beshogeg, bein bemezid,
bein bedibur, bein bema'aseh,
bein bemachashava, bein behirhur,
bein begilgul zeh, bein begilgul acher,
l'chal bar Yisrael' velo ye'anesh shum adam besibati.

Yehi ratzon milfanecha,
Adonai Elohai vElohei avotai,
shelo echeta od,
umah shechatati lefanecha,
mechok berachamecha harabim,
aval lo al yedei yesorim vocholayim ra'im.
Yehiyu leratzon imrei fi vehegyon libi lefanecha,
Adonai Tzuri veGo'ali.

Master of the universe,
I hereby forgive each person who angered
or antagonized me, or sinned against me—
whether against my body or my property,
my honor or anything of mine,
whether accidentally or willfully, carelessly or purposely,
whether by speech or deed, thought or fantasy,
whether in this incarnation or in another incarnation,
—may no one be punished because of me.

May it be Your will, Adonai my God and God of my ancestors,
that I may sin no more.
Whatever my error before You,
may it be blotted out in Your abundant mercies,
but not through suffering or severe illness.
May the expressions of my mouth
and the thoughts of my heart
be pleasing to You,
Adonai, my Rock and my Redeemer.

2. Forgiving Yourself

Lie down in your bed. Enjoy the horizontal position of rest and the surren-der of tension you can sense in your body. Take a moment to feel good about yourself for finishing a day to the best of your ability.

As you gaze around your sukkah of peace, a warm breeze gently blows open one of the curtains and reveals a magnificent garden glowing in the moonlight. Imagine that you rise and walk out into the garden, discover-ing that it is lit with fireflies. It is as if angels surround you with lanterns of God's light. As you look around the garden, you see that the flowers are lit from underneath, and their colors are vibrant against the blue-black of the night. As you walk, you step on a shimmering stone pathway that leads you to the center of the garden.

All is well. The sounds of night awaken your ears. You hear crickets and the sound of the breeze. Notice the sound of your own breath, your own heartbeat, and your footsteps. With each step, the breeze sweeps your body gently, cleansing away any remnants of the day that just ended. You feel the breeze clean your scalp and your mind...your throat, heart, arms, hands, and fingertips...your solar plexus, your belly, your pelvis, your groin...your legs, your feet. A warm breeze blows down through your whole spine, cleansing each vertebra from top to bottom.

You now come to the center of the garden, where there is a place for you to sit next to a reflecting pool. As you sit down, peer into the pool and see your image. Do not judge what you see there. Know that it may be just a vague outline or shadow. Seeing yourself is not easy. Ask God to reveal to you the image that God sees. Try to be gentle and non-critical. This is essential for your healing.

Notice how you feel, and how you have been treating yourself. Gently ask: How have I harmed myself? Have I harmed my body? My posses-sions? My honor or self-esteem? Have I hurt myself through relationships with family or friends? Have I done it accidentally or willfully?

What do you feel guilty or angry about in the deepest core of your being? You must try to focus on only one small aspect of yourself that you want to forgive—one place of disappointment or anger, pity, doubt, or guilt. This is your hardest task because self-criticism can stop the healing process. Use your most loving self to focus on the place that is hurting the most right now.

Try to name the feeling that you feel toward yourself. For example, "I feel angry at myself for working at a job that never let me grow." "I feel guilty that I wasn't a more involved parent." "I feel disappointed in myself about my smoking habit (or your eating or drinking habits, etc.)." "I feel frustrated that I continually doubt myself."

Now that you have named it, ask God to help you stop hurting yourself. Know that you are not bad, that you are only human, and that mistakes are how we learn.

Look again into the pool before you. See your reflection being washed with a shower of light that comes from the moon. The light falls on the sur-face of the pool like a mist, then melts into a healing salve. Dip your hand into the salve and coat those areas of your body where you feel the pain.

Let the warmth of healing dissolve into your body. Notice that downy-soft wings now surround you, holding and comforting you as you say, "Ribbono shel olam, Master of the universe, I for-give myself to you. Help me accept myself and learn from my mistakes. Show me my lesson. Help me hold myself in my own wings of acceptance and inner love."

Breathe. Sit silently for a moment. Look into the reflecting pool now and see your image shining back at you with joy and light. Your image thanks you, and you respond by thanking God for helping you find the courage to do this work. Slowly you stand and walk back from the garden on the moonlit path. Your sukkah *of peace opens again, and you slip into your warm bed. Now you can rest. Say the forgiveness prayer for yourself:*

Ribbono shel olam, I hereby forgive myself
for what I have done that blemished my Divine image,
whether my body, my mind, my self-esteem,
whether accidentally or willfully, in this incarnation or another.

May it be Your will,
Adonai my God and God of my ancestors,
that I may sin no more.
Whatever my error before You,
may it be blotted out in Your abundant mercies,
but not through suffering or severe illness.
May the words of my mouth and the thoughts of my heart
be pleasing to You,
Adonai, my Rock and my Redeemer.

רִבּוֹנוֹ שֶׁל עוֹלָם,
הֲרֵינִי מוֹחֵל ⁄ מוֹחֶלֶת לִי

Ribbono shel olam
hareni mochel/mochelet li.

Master of the universe,
I hereby forgive myself.

3. Asking Forgiveness from Another Person

Rest in the comfort of your bed. Look around at your beautiful sukkah *of peace. Imagine it as elegant or as simple as you wish. It is your place of peace and rest. Enjoy the feeling of resting on the horizontal plane, a position to receive healing.*

One side of your sukkah *opens and reveals a warm moonlit beach. A warm breeze gently guides you down a shimmering path of light that leads you to the beach. The sand is cool underneath your feet, and a warm blanket like angels' wings covers your shoulders. The sound of the waves is melodic and the breeze sings along. You hear your own heartbeat as the bass, and your breath weaves the small symphony together.*

The breeze cleanses your body by dusting away any impurities you may have picked up during the day. Your scalp tingles as the wind combs your hair. The breeze moves through your throat and heart, arms and hands. It cleanses your belly and groin, and your legs and feet. Little gusts of wind blow through your spine, cleansing each vertebra from top to bottom. You open your arms wide and enjoy the freedom you feel from the inside out.

As you look out over the ocean, you humbly ask God to help you find one person you need to ask for forgiveness, who is in pain from something you did.

Be as gentle and loving toward yourself as possible. Honor yourself for having the courage to do this work. When the person appears before your inner vision, think about what you have done to him or her that needs for-giveness. Name it. For example, "I replaced you with another friend, and I know that I hurt you." "I lied to protect myself and what happened as a result hurt you." "I criticized you and those words caused you pain. I'm sorry." "I frightened you with my actions."

You don't know whether the other person will forgive you in ordinary life, but you now have begun the process by becoming clear about your responsibility for what happened, and by stating your good intent.

Now see a silver strand of light connecting your heart and solar plexus with that of the other person. Feel how powerful the energy is that is being drained from you because of what has been going on between the two of you. Now say, "Please forgive me." Repeat these words if you feel the need to do so. "Please forgive me."

Take a deep breath. Notice that the cord between you has a knot. Reach out and untie it. See the cord that attaches to the other person coil back-slowly toward his or her heart. You may want to visualize yourself placing your hand over the other person's heart, gently massaging it to help the healing.

Now see that your end of the cord is spiraling back to you, making a warm, healing circle around your heart and solar plexus. It continues to move through your whole body, helping your body, mind, and soul unite.

As you now look at the other person, know that you have begun to set him or her free from this painful attachment. Do not expect the other per-son to receive, appreciate, or reject what you have done. You have done your own work with God. Wish the other person well.

Look up at the stars twinkling as they send you a shower of hope, joy, and renewal. You become aware of the warm breeze caressing your body, the sound of the waves, and the cool sand under foot. You walk back to your sukkah *of peace. The curtains open and you slip under your warm covers, prepared for a good sleep.*

Now say the last part of the forgiveness prayer:

Ribbono shel olam, I hereby ask Your forgiveness.
May it be your will, Adonai my God and
God of my ancestors, that I may sin no more.

Whatever my error before You,
may it be blotted out in Your abundant mercies,
but not through suffering or severe illness.
May the words of my mouth and the thoughts of my heart
be pleasing to You,
Adonai, my Rock and my Redeemer.

שְׁמַע יִשְׂרָאֵל, יהוה אֱלֹהֵינוּ, יהוה אֶחָד:
בָּרוּךְ שֵׁם כְּבוֹד מַלְכוּתוֹ לְעוֹלָם וָעֶד.

וְאָהַבְתָּ אֵת יהוה אֱלֹהֶיךָ,
בְּכָל־לְבָבְךָ, וּבְכָל־נַפְשְׁךָ, וּבְכָל־מְאֹדֶךָ.
וְהָיוּ הַדְּבָרִים הָאֵלֶּה, אֲשֶׁר אָנֹכִי מְצַוְּךָ הַיּוֹם,
עַל־לְבָבֶךָ:
וְשִׁנַּנְתָּם לְבָנֶיךָ,
וְדִבַּרְתָּ בָּם,
בְּשִׁבְתְּךָ בְּבֵיתֶךָ,
וּבְלֶכְתְּךָ בַדֶּרֶךְ,
וּבְשָׁכְבְּךָ, וּבְקוּמֶךָ:
וּקְשַׁרְתָּם לְאוֹת עַל־יָדֶךָ,
וְהָיוּ לְטֹטָפֹת בֵּין עֵינֶיךָ:
וּכְתַבְתָּם עַל־מְזֻזוֹת
בֵּיתֶךָ וּבִשְׁעָרֶיךָ:

Hear, O Israel, Adonai is Our God, Adonai is One!
Blessed be the Name of the Glory of his Kingdom forever.

You shall love Adonai your God with all your heart,
and with all your soul, and with all your resources.
These words that I command you today
shall be upon your heart.
You shall teach them diligently to your children,
and speak of them
when you are sitting in your house,
when you are walking on the road,
and when you lie down, and when you rise up.
You shall bind them as a sign upon your hand,
and they will be as reminders between your eyes,
and you shall write them on the doorposts
of your house and on your gates.

4

Shema:
Listening to Infinity—
The Gift of Michael

AS JACOB WAS ABOUT TO DIE, he called his sons to him and
was about to tell them what would befall them in the end of
days. Then the *Shekhinah* [Divine Presence] left him. "Alas!"
he said, "perhaps one of my children has a flaw. After all, Abraham had an Ishmael, Isaac had an Esau."

His sons all answered, "*Shema Yisrael, Adonai Elohenu,
Adonai Echad!*—Just as God is One in your heart, so God is
One in ours."

Jacob opened his mouth and exclaimed, "*Baruch shem kevod
malchuto leolam va'ed*—Blessed is the Name of the Glory of
his Kingdom forever!"

—Talmud *Pesachim* 56a

How the Shema Guards Our Doorways

The *Shema Yisrael* is the most famous prayer in Judaism. It is the prayer that marks our most profound movements between one state of being and another. It is a prayer of doorways—and so it is inscribed on our doorposts. Here are some examples of how the *Shema* is used:

- ☐ Jews are commanded to say the entire *Shema* twice daily, at the opening and the closing of the day.

- ☐ The first line—*Shema Yisrael, Adonai Elohenu, Adonai Echad*—is recited aloud in the synagogue, just after taking the Torah scrolls from the Ark before Torah readings. This is the moment when the Torah emerges into public view.

- ☐ The first line is recited at the climax of Yom Kippur, at the end of the evening *Ne'ilah* service—the service of the "closing of the gates."

- ☐ It is considered a great thing if a person dies with the words of *Shema Yisrael* on his or her lips. It marks the doorway between life and death.

- ☐ Some Jews recite the *Shema* over a newborn baby boy the night before his circumcision, which is his first rite of passage.

- ☐ The *Shema* is inscribed on the *mezuzah*, which is placed on the doorposts of Jewish houses and gates.

- ☐ It is written in the *tefillin*, whose boxes and straps connect head and heart.

The *Shema* points to the heart of Judaism. It is a profound way to walk with God through the doorways of our lives and toward transformation.

Most commentaries also explain that the *Shema* is a great formulation of the Jewish creed. According to the great medieval legal scholar and philosopher, Maimonides, the *Shema* enables us to fulfill the command to affirm the Oneness of God, and the love of God, both of which are foundational for all Jewish belief and practice.[1] But if this were only an intellectual matter, why would we need the specific verbal formula of *Shema Yisrael, Adonai Elohenu, Adonai Echad*? Why would it be so prominent on our "doorways"? We could just state, "There is only one God, and we are commanded to love our Creator."

Another way of asking this question is to look at the unique ritual that surrounds the *Shema*. Why do we say, "Hear! Listen!" Why do we use two expressions for the one God—the four-letter name pronounced "*Adonai*" and the name "*Elohim*" with the possessive "our," *Elohenu*? Why do we cover our eyes with our right hand while reciting it, and why do we extend the word *Echad*, "One," while making sure to say the "d" sound clearly at the end? Why do we follow these words in an undertone with another phrase that does not occur in the Torah or, indeed, the whole Hebrew Bible, *Baruch shem kevod malchuto leolam va'ed*, "Blessed be the Name of the Glory of Kingdom forever"?

To answer these questions, let's start with the first word, *Shema*, meaning "Hear."

Listening for God's Voice

Shema. The command "Hear" calls attention to a sensory rather than an intellectual process. At the same time, the word *shema* carries a number of connotations in Hebrew. It also means "understand," "accept," and "witness." The medieval mystic Abulafia said that its letters signify "Lift your eyes upward."[2] So the command invites us to a multidimensional experience.

Rabbi Yitzchak Ginzburgh expands on the meaning of each of the letters.[3] The *shin* represents a flame attached to a coal, which represents the change that appears to emerge from a changeless essence. The words that we hear and their vibration are part of a world of change, but they are connected to a place of timelessness.

The *mem*'s comforting hum represents water or consciousness, specifically the fount of Divine wisdom that comes through Torah. Try breathing as you say *shema*, inhaling on the "sh" sound and exhaling with the "ma." Repeat this a few times. You will notice that it sounds very much like the breathing we do when we are swimming. So the word *shema* asks us to swim in the waters of higher consciousness.

The *ayin* represents the eye of Divine Providence, an infinite awareness beyond human sight. It hints that sight is raised to another level, beyond the limited and analytical way we usually use our eyes, by being included in the spectrum of "hearing." *Ayin* can also be read as *ein*, which means "nothing." The great No-thing-ness, the Infinite that can be compared to no-thing, lies beyond the boundaries of ordinary consciousness.

The different meanings of the word, and the hints about these that come through its letters, tell us that the "hearing" alluded to in the *Shema* is far more profound than what we usually think of when we hear the telephone ring or we turn on the radio. We are called to our faith with the word "hear" in order to focus on the vibrations picked up by the ears, which involves us in different ways than our other senses.

The commentators on the *Shema* have especially emphasized the difference between hearing and sight. It is more than simply attending to a different set of wavelengths. Our ears pick up information from all around us, rather than from just in front, as our eyes do. Sight, because it focuses forward, asks us to look for a path. It tends to emphasize boundaries, whereas hearing is more open-ended. We can listen to several things at one time if they are not offering conflicting information. For example, I can—all at the same time—hear my daughter speaking on the phone, hear music in the background, and hear the fan that is blowing cool air behind me. The ears invite us not so much toward a path as toward a totality that blends each individual item that the ear senses.

Further, because hearing is connected with vibrations on the tympanum, it works directly with other senses, like the sense of touch or the inner kinesthetic sense. We can use these senses to feel the vibration of voice in one's own or another's throat and chest. Hearing in this broader sense is not only with the ears. Our ears can pick up nuances of tone and expression that convey emotions, even when we cannot see the face of the person speaking.

This reminds us of another connotation of *shema*: "understand." Understanding is hearing more deeply and completely. This is even more important than hearing with the physical ears. *Halakhah* (Jewish law) specifies that we must read the *Shema* audibly in order to hear ourselves say it. But according to the sages of the Talmud, if we forget to recite it audibly, our obligation is still fulfilled because the emphasis is on understanding. We might be meditating on the meaning of the words, and therefore forget to say it audibly. We are supposed to read the *Shema* in Hebrew if possible, but it is permitted to read it in any language that we understand.

The focus on understanding is also clear from the traditional interpretation of the famous words of the Jewish people upon receiving the Torah: *Na'aseh v'nishmah* (Exodus 24:7) which literally means "We will do and we will hear." That hardly makes sense—how can we do something before we hear it? But as the rabbis explained, *nishmah* means "we will understand"—we will obey and do the *mitzvot* of the Torah, and then we will study so we can understand them better.

Most importantly, understanding involves bringing the words of the *Shema* into our very being—as the first paragraph of the *Shema* says, "place these words on your heart." Hearing-as-understanding is deep and personal. In contrast, the analytical faculty of knowing is more closely connected to the sense of sight. Thus, when we follow someone's argument to a conclusion, we say, "I see." But when we grasp the nuances and emotional quality of someone's statement, we might say, "Yes, I hear you."

When the Torah says "hear" rather than "see," it is not merely implying that God has no visible form, but rather that we should understand at a deeper level. Hearing is the ability to understand non-judgmentally and absorb at the soul level—to hear the person, not just the content. This is illustrated in a story about King Solomon, who asked God to "give Your servant an understanding heart"—literally a *lev shomea*, or "hearing heart" (1 Kings 3:5–12). He needed this so he could listen to people's complaints and legal cases, and deal with them wisely. We truly hear with our hearts.[4]

Another fascinating point about sound is that it theoretically never ends. The sound produced at the beginning of the known universe—the "Big Bang" as science calls it—is still perceptible as background radiation of a certain wavelength. The tuning fork vibrates for a long time before friction finally causes it to cease, but the waves that it started continue on indefinitely. As the Chief Rabbi of Trier once taught, "Since what is heard is the least dimensional, it is easier to imagine it as something unlimited and extendible into infinity, than what is visible or tactile."[5] This is what we suggested above with regard to the letter *ayin*, the No-thing-ness that goes beyond all boundaries. Thus, the mystics of Jewish tradition said that we are always standing at Sinai, where we "saw no form" but heard God's voice (Deuteronomy 4:12–19). Through our sense of hearing, we can always tune into the Presence of God.

And the experience of that Presence is to be a personal experience. In the Torah scroll, two letters of the first line are written large: the *ayin* of *Shema* and the *dalet* of *Echad*. These two letters spell *ed*, or "witness." A witness has to have a personal experience of the event to which he or she is testifying. This alludes to the idea that in saying the *Shema*, we are testifying to something that we deeply know and understand to be true.

The fact that we say the *Shema* and normally hear our own voice saying it adds another dimension. Our vocal vibration extends out and back. This can remind us of the phenomenon of echo-location in dolphins and porpoises. The "radar" that they possess to pick up vibrations—because their eyes are small and not so reliable—depends on sounds bouncing back to them from distant objects. When we say the *Shema*, we can imagine our voice vibrating out to Infinity, and bouncing back. It can simultaneously give us a sense of our distance from God and of our eternal connection to God.

Beginning our declaration of faith with the *Shema* thus involves a complex and profound act. We hear our voice, and project it; we are asked to listen and to understand. Hearing has the potential to become an act of the complete person. It can bring together our ears, our sense of vibration, our ability to "hear" ourselves and respond to others, our intellectual ability to grasp and assent to an idea, an understanding that comes from the heart, and a yearning to reach toward God.

If all this is implied in the simple word "hear," it opens up many other questions. How are we to develop this level of depth and commitment? How can we come to our own recital of the *Shema* with a higher consciousness? We can begin by looking at the ways the *Shema* has been spoken in the past. We will look at three different contexts. One is the *Shema* as an experience of extremes, like the *Shema* at the end of Yom Kippur or at the end of life. Another is the *Shema* in the context of a community. The third is the *Shema* embedded in our lives, as natural as the breath we take.

The Awesome *Shema* of Rabbi Akiva

The man who most embodies the *Shema* as total devotion and commitment to God, who died with the words of the *Shema* on his lips, is Rabbi Akiva. A sage of the second century, he lived and died during the period of severe Roman oppression that reached a peak during the Jewish revolt led by Bar Kochba in 132–135 C.E. Akiva was the epitome of the *baal teshuvah* (someone who returns to Judaism). He awoke to his mission late in life, at the age of forty, when he met his future wife, Rachel, while working as a simple shepherd. She convinced him to devote himself to Torah study. Rabbi Akiva was one of the early codifiers of the oral law,[6] and he became known not only for his legal opinions but also for his mystical teachings. He is famous for his statement, "'Love your neighbor as yourself' (Leviticus 19:18). This is the main point of the whole Torah."[7]

During the period preceding the Bar Kochba revolt, the Roman government forbade the teaching of Torah and Rabbi Akiva was arrested. One of his supporters asked why he had continued to teach when he knew he was putting himself in danger. He replied that for a Jew to go without Torah is like a fish trying to swim out of the water. Torah had become his entire life.

The Romans killed Akiva by lacerating his flesh with hot combs. During his torture, he turned to his students and said that all his life he had been reciting the passage from the *Shema*: "You shall love your God with all your heart, with all your soul, and with all your strength," but he had never known what it meant to say "with all your soul." Now he knew that it meant "even if your soul [*nefesh*, life-force] is taken from you." As he died, he slowly extended the word *Echad*, One. Thus, until his last moment, he maintained consciousness, not allowing body and soul to split to relieve his pain, but living even the pain to its fullest for the sake of God.[8]

The extraordinary story of Rabbi Akiva points to an important aspect of the *Shema*. We all have certain doorways in our life that are difficult to cross, and where we are tempted to split body and soul from each other. We may want to put God away in a compartment, to be taken out only on proper occasions. We may want to indulge in the physical in order to seek oblivion from pain. The *Shema* asks us to hold the two together, to take God into the pain with us, and to live with it.

Each of us has the responsibility to face and address what threatens or frightens us in our own lives, and to embody the *Shema* in the face of those threats. Each of us must ask, What is the ultimate pain for me? Is it a life-threatening disease? The pain of a loved one? The death of a beloved? A child with a disorder? Loss of job or career? Infertility? Addiction? Bankruptcy? A change that might disrupt my life or that of my loved ones? Each of us has a unique life situation and our own unique suffering in the world. The story of Rabbi Akiva can remind us that our pain may reveal how God wants to work through us. Akiva would have been great even if he had not died a terrible death. But his death sealed what he had done in a way that would never be forgotten, not by those who saw him die and not for millennia to come.

Akiva wanted to stay attached to Torah. He could stay in his body and swim in the consciousness of God through the vehicle of the *Shema*. When we also find a way to let go of the rewards and securities the world has to offer, we may feel the words of the *Shema* sounding sweetly on our lips. Affirming the Oneness of reality is the ultimate message. When we can begin to internalize this, we, like Rabbi Akiva, can go through life with a growing faith.

Try this exercise: Write your own "Rabbi Akiva" story, using the circumstances of your life as the test that puts you through the flames. Include your own victorious ending to the story.

Becoming One Family

The second way that the *Shema* is said is as part of a community. Rather than an individual in his ultimate moment with God, we see others around us, saying the *Shema* with us. The words themselves assert this: We say "Hear, O Israel" as the preface to asserting the Oneness of God because Judaism is about people more than doctrine. *Yisrael*, or "Israel," emphasizes the reality of people in a community who are engaged in this action and directing themselves toward more conscious listening and deeper understanding. It is about a heritage of commitment through the ages, reaching back through grandparents and great-grandparents, through lineage branching out from one country to the next, back through millennia to ancestors in an ancient land.

Israel is the name of one of our ancestors, Jacob. He is the last of the three patriarchs, combining in himself the qualities of his father and grandfather. He brought their efforts to a culmination by being the father of the twelve tribes and settling in the land that would be named after him. He acquired the name Israel after wrestling with an angel. Israel can be understood to mean "Wrestler with God." By transposing letters, it can also mean "Song of God." Mystical traditions portray the Throne of God as having Jacob's face engraved upon it, for he was the culmination of the effort to recreate humans in God's image since Adam's fall. When we say "Hear, O Israel," we can imagine ourselves speaking to our holy ancestors, telling them that we are continuing, with as much faith and clarity as we can, the great tradition that they established for us.

> As Jacob was about to die, he called his sons to him and was about to tell them what would befall them in the end of days. Then the *Shekhinah* [Divine Presence] left him. "Alas!" he said, "perhaps one of my children has a flaw. After all, Abraham had an Ishmael, Isaac had an Esau."
>
> His sons all answered, *"Shema Yisrael, Adonai Elohenu, Adonai Echad!—*Just as God is One in your heart, so God is One in ours."
>
> Jacob opened his mouth and exclaimed, *"Baruch shem kevod malchuto leolam va'ed—*Blessed is the Name of the Glory of his Kingdom forever!"
>
> —Talmud *Pesachim* 56a

At this point in the story, Jacob is on his deathbed and at the edge of consciousness. As a supremely righteous person, he has access to *ruach hakodesh*, the Holy Spirit, which is about to give him a prophetic vision of *yamim achronim*, which is usually translated as "the end of days," or "future times." He says, "Come near, and I will tell you what will befall you in the latter days. Gather round me and listen, you sons of Jacob, listen to Israel your father" (Genesis 49:1–2). Then, our tradition says—though this is not in the biblical text—the vision departs. Some say that an angel informed Jacob that he was not allowed to reveal the vision, and so it was taken away. Others say that the capacity for prophecy returned to him after his sons recited the *Shema* and he responded with *Baruch shem kevod malchuto leolam va'ed*.

What is the midrashic tradition telling us about what is happening

who brought you here. Live your life out of love for God, and keep all these things on your heart.

The Jewish people were not being asked to die for God but to live for God. God would be their beacon of light as they looked back at their past and as they marched forward. This is a different aspect of the *Shema*: a beacon that illuminates one's life. But it also connects to the first paragraph of the *Shema*: "You shall love the Lord your God with all your heart, with all your soul and with all your strength .... You shall teach them diligently to your children, and you shall speak of them when you are sitting in your house, when you are walking on the road." This is love that can be cultivated daily and as regularly as breathing.

How can we bring God as Love—and our love for God—into the ordinary moments of our lives, moments when we are not in extreme circumstances, not facing a challenge, and not feeling particularly connected to our heritage or our community? This aspect of the *Shema* is the aspect of faith, the certainty that God is always with us. Rabbi Nachman of Breslov emphasizes that the bedtime *Shema* is a prayer of faith. When we go to sleep, we do not have clear knowledge based on sense perception, but rather faith, based on willingness to let go and trust. This faith comes from the "Light of the Face" of God, which is connected with night and with the moon. It is also connected to the "seventy faces of Torah," the various ways that different people study and understand Torah. Divine teaching comes to us in a garment that is our own particular way of receiving Divine Light.[12]

Imagine that you have a private screening room, where you can run the movie of your life whenever you want. You can stop and view different pictures, skip around, and jump into past events you have heard about. You can even call up images of the future you would like to create. This screening room is your opening into the *Shema* prayer. The imagery is all on the software; the *Shema* is the light that puts it on the screen before you.

What images from your life would you call up on screen to imagine Oneness? What calls to you with the feeling of going "home"? What expresses deep, abiding love? Think of your favorite music or work of art, your favorite natural scenery or meal. Call up images from history— the splitting of the sea, standing at Sinai, Masada, the Western Wall in Jerusalem. Or from geography—Big Sur, the Grand Canyon, Yosemite Valley, Niagara Falls. What are the places where your heart sings?

Where do you find a Promised Land? Where do you feel love?

The answers to these questions give you the frames you can call up when you say the *Shema* in your ordinary daily life. It is not a prayer in extremis, but a prayer you can breathe, naturally. "God is One.... You shall love." Loving life, loving people, loving your sleep and your dreams, and trusting in faith—all these are other aspects of the *Shema*.

The two aspects—the extreme and the ordinary, Rabbi Akiva and the Jewish people on the plains of Moab—are embodied in the *Shema* itself. The first is encoded in the name for God spelled Y-H-V-H (*Yud-Heh-Vav-Heh*) and pronounced *Adonai*. This is the name of God transcendent, reaching down to earth in mercy. The second is hinted by the name *Elohim*. This is God in nature, God in the ordinary, God in the plural, God in natural and karmic forces, God as judgment and source of regulation and standards.

All these, the *Shema* says, are One.

Unifying the Higher and Lower Worlds

Now we can understand one of the great mystical teachings about the *Shema*. The main point of the first line of the *Shema* is to stress the Oneness of God. However, in Jewish teaching this is not simply a doctrinal affirmation reminding us of important beliefs. Said with *kavannah* (intent), it actually has an effect. The mystics called this *Yichud Hashem*, literally the "union of God." In English, it is usually referred to as the Divine Unification. It is as if human acts actually reunite God with him/herself, so to speak, and help unite the world with God.

But this does not happen automatically. It requires us to make the effort to unify ourselves, to concentrate our being into saying the words. It requires us to meditate. Indeed, this is one of the rare occasions in Judaism when meditation—or, more precisely, contemplation—is part of the requirement of the *mitzvah*.[13]

Adonai Elohenu, "Y-H-V-H our God." The words here immediately reveal a problem. The *Shema*, which is about the unity of God, uses two names of God. Why would this be the case in a prayer that is intended to affirm unity? And why, out of the several names used for God in

Torah, would these be chosen? The reason is that each name has its own specific connotations, and the connotations of these two names are, for the most part, diametrically opposed to each other. The first name is the four-letter name, or tetragrammaton, Y-H-V-H, which was revealed to Moses in Egypt. We do not actually pronounce these letters, but instead substitute *Adonai*, which literally means "my Master." This name is normally associated with God as a force that acts redemptively in history. It is connected especially to the particular and unique relationship God has with the Jewish people as a personal and merciful deity. *Adonai* announces that God is not abstract and distant, but is deeply related to the human world.

Elohenu is the first-person-plural possessive ("our") of *Elohim*. It literally means "gods" but is usually translated as "God." This name of God is associated with Divinity as it manifests impersonally in nature and universally to all peoples. God here is a judge who upholds natural and moral law. These two names are encountered repeatedly in Scripture and tradition, yet they are clearly opposed to each other:

Adonai	*Elohim*
God in history	God in nature
Particular	Universal
Personal	Impersonal
Mercy	Judgment

By placing them both in the *Shema*, the Torah is stating that despite our sense of the differences between them, they are really one. Moreover, it suggests that the way we usually perceive reality—as black and white, male and female, good and evil—is really quite a limited perspective. As Rabbi Norman Lamm has written, "All such dichotomies and distinctions are purely subjective, expressive of our human limitations. Beyond all such divisions there is but one objective Reality." [14]

Adonai Echad, the next phrase, means "Y-H-V-H is One." This is the place where, according to most understandings of the *halakhah* (Jewish law) about the *Shema*, we should meditate deeply on the meaning of what we are saying in this prayer. The last syllable of the word *Echad* is prolonged in order to allow specifically for contemplation. The actual content of the contemplation, which many commentators have discussed at length, involves how we understand the principal meanings of our affirmation of Oneness. Over time, we can develop and deepen our understanding and our meditation.

At the most basic level, *Echad* means that there is one God and not many. Tradition tells us that the revelation of this truth was granted to Abraham and through his lineage to the Jewish people, and that eventually the whole world will accept this truth. Indeed, we find that many religions, even when they appear to worship many deities, have a concept of a single Creator or a monistic entity that is behind all the multiplicity of life. As it says in the *Alenu* prayer recited at the end of every synagogue prayer service, "In that day the Lord will be One and his Name One"—eventually all will recognize that there is only one to be called God. Thus, while saying *Echad*, we can contemplate the spread of the idea of one Creator, one Reality, to the entire human race.

In addition, Oneness means that God is sovereign over all. There is nothing outside God's purview. One suggestion for this meditation is that "One should prolong the [syllable of] *dalet* while meditating that the Creator of the world is king above and below, in heaven and on earth and its four corners, east and west and north and south, in the great abyss, and in his own 248 organs." Rav Kook adds that as we say the *chet* syllable we should meditate on God's sovereignty over all time because the letter *chet* is also the number eight, which stands for eternity and what is beyond human time.[15]

Further, the "unification" that is accomplished in the prayer suggests an intimate union. *Yichud Hashem*, the term for the affirmation of the unity of God, actually means "union of God," not "unity." The emphasis is on an inner or internal unity, a true "union" implying that we cannot separate the components that have been united. God's various aspects are truly One.

The Oneness and Uniqueness of God also mean that the Divine is incomparable and unknowable. Some of the mystics have held that nothing else but God truly exists.[16] Practically speaking, the unknowable quality of God's Oneness has been interpreted to mean that when we say the first line of the *Shema*, we are affirming something that is actually beyond our comprehension. The Zohar refers to the recitation of *Shema Yisrael* as the "Higher Unification." We are reaching for something beyond our ken, trying to move in our meditations to a more elevated perspective than we normally can see. Our thoughts travel from this world to the highest world, a world of unity and comprehensiveness. Rabbi Lamm interprets this as an all-inclusive contemplation: "We include ourselves along with human souls, with all things living and inanimate, with all the worlds both astronomical and spiritual—in an awesome and loving fellowship of all existence, elevating them with us to the One, the Cause of all Causes." When all is one, we are not alone. When all is one, we can be present in the moment and aware of a complete and full reality.

Mystics called the second line, *Baruch shem kevod malchuto leolam va'ed*, the "Lower Unification." The letters of the word *va'ed* could be transmuted, according to one system of working with Hebrew letters, into the word *Echad*, thus also signifying unity. If the *Shema Yisrael* moves our thoughts upward, the *Baruch shem* goes in the opposite direction: "We draw down . . . the influx of his will . . . his love from its source in the ineffable Name ["the Lord"] to this world . . . we draw down the Ancient of Ancients to be with and unite with us here"[17] This unification relates to this world of space and time rather than to the mysterious and unknowable world of the Divine. It says that the Glory of God is not distant, but here and now. In each specific entity and experience of our world, Oneness is present.

Historically, the addition of this line is interesting, for it occurs nowhere in the *Tanach* (Torah, Prophets, and Writings). Apparently, it was used instead of "Amen" during Yom Kippur services in the Holy Temple in Jerusalem. For 2,000 years at least, it has been said as the second line of the *Shema*. It is said in an undertone except on Yom Kippur, when it is said aloud. A midrash tells us that Moses overheard the angels using the phrase, and brought it down for the Jewish people. But another tradition ascribes it to the patriarch Jacob on his deathbed, as we saw in the passage from the Talmud at the beginning of this chapter.

Clearly, *Baruch shem* is meant to parallel the *Shema*, for it also contains six words. It literally means "Blessed is the Name of the Glory of his Kingdom forever." The Zohar associates the various parts of these two lines with the story of the creation of the world.[18] The sequence of the words itself—Name . . . Glory . . . Kingdom—suggests a series of levels: We are not praising God directly, nor the Divine Kingdom, nor its Glory. Instead, we are celebrating the Name of its Glory. *Baruch shem* suggests a series of mirrors or reflections, each more cloudy than the next, through which we see Divinity.

Still, we can "see" God in the world that is before us, and so we say
Baruch shem. To be able to see Godliness in the midst of the finite world
is a great gift. It means that our connection to the world and to God is so
deep that the two are not really separate for us. When we perceive the
world from such a perspective, subject and object do not really exist, and
everything shines with Divinity. Rav Kook suggests that the *Baruch
shem* is said quietly because displaying our awareness of this unity pub-
licly would be boastful. Instead, we can quietly, not ostentatiously, help
others realize the truth of this revelation.[19]

We may not be able to accept or hold all these aspects of Oneness in
our minds while we say the *Shema*. But they can be inspirations to us
and can serve as goals to be sought in our spiritual development. When
we cannot feel Oneness in our life, we can still study and learn about it
through the words of Torah—to "speak of them when we sit in our
houses and walk on the road."

Love in the *Shema*

"You shall love your God with all your heart, with all your soul, and
with all your resources." The first paragraph of the *Shema* focuses on
love—the love of human beings for God. In the regular daily service,
the *Shema* is preceded by a statement of God's love for human beings
and for the Jewish people: "You have taught us Your Torah .... Blessed
are You, *Adonai*, who has chosen the people Israel with love." The word
for "love" in Hebrew, *ahavah*, has a numerical value of thirteen, which
is the same as the numerical value of the word *echad*, "One."

What does it mean to love and be loved by God? The sages brought up
the point that this is presented as a command. How can love be commanded? Isn't it spontaneous? We might begin by saying that love is
not so much a feeling as a state of being. Emotions color our experience, but most of them are based on past physical experiences, a kind
of knee-jerk reaction that we impose on new experience. Since God, by
definition, is not like any other experience, we cannot adequately
approach our relationship to God in terms of our past emotions.

So, the sages tell us, this love is something to be developed. First of all, it is possible to develop a love for God by studying and meditating on Torah. The first paragraph of the *Shema* states this explicitly: Study Torah ("put these words on your heart"); speak words of Torah frequently wherever you are; say them morning and night (specifically the *Shema*); teach them to your children; wear *tefillin* and put *mezuzahs* on your doors. Surround yourself with Torah and you will evoke the love of God that is hidden in your heart.

Second, love can grow through action. When an infant is born, parents often feel an immediate connection with their new child, a connection that grows and deepens over the next few weeks. This "bonding" happens through all the acts of caring that the parents perform for the child: feeding and clothing him, tucking her in with blankets, rocking and singing at bedtime. Similarly, the sages insist that by loving our fellow creatures we learn to love God. As God provided an earth on which living creatures can grow, we can care for the earth, for its plants and animals and, most of all, for other human beings. The more we become involved in such actions with an awareness of the Creator who designed this amazing place, the stronger our bonds with God will be. Maimonides taught that meditating on the great and wondrous creations of God and seeing in them the infinite and incomparable wisdom of the Divine will bring a person to love and praise God, and be filled with a yearning to know God.[20]

The author of the *Tanya*, Rabbi Schneur Zalman of Liadi, wrote that this kind of love is called *ahavat olam*, "eternal love," which

> ... comes from the understanding and knowledge of the greatness of God, the blessed *En Sof* [Endless One], Who fills all worlds and encompasses all worlds and before Whom everything is accounted as nothing at all .... For as a result of such contemplation the attribute of love that is in the soul ... will not desire anything whatever in the world other than God alone, the Source of the vitality of all enjoyments .... As is written: "Whom have I in heaven [but Thee]? And there is nothing upon earth that I desire with thee. My flesh and my heart yearn, O Rock of my heart." [21]

There is also a kind of love called *ahavah rabbah*, or "great love," which comes from someone who has perfect awe of God. It can be experienced even when life is not going the way we might wish. The Zohar says that even suffering is designed to bring forth love. Otherwise we might have only the kind of love that emerges in good circumstances:

> Perfect love is the kind that remains steadfast in both phases, whether of affliction or prosperity. The right way of loving one's Master is expressed in the traditional teaching that says, "even if he deprives you of your life" [as in "with all your soul"]. This is, then, perfect love, embracing two phases. It was for this reason that the light of creation that first emerged was afterward withdrawn. When it was withdrawn suffering emerged, in order that there might be this perfect love.[22]

Each of these types of love has many shades and gradations, according to each individual's capacity and effort. No one can know where another person is in respect to these qualities.

These understandings of love hint at various aspects of the connection we might feel, at one time or another, to God. When we see the hand of the Creator in the grandeur of nature, or when we study the way the human body works, we can feel a yearning for greater connection to our Source. When we see people inspired by their faith to persevere in the face of adversity, we can recognize something deep within that keeps pulling us toward love of God. Beyond this, says Rabbi Schneur Zalman, there is also a simpler kind of love, one that every Jewish person has inherited from their ancestors. It has aspects of both *ahavat olam* and *ahavah rabbah*. He describes this as "My soul, I desire You," which means that we long for and love God just as we desire our own life and our own deepest vitality.

This hidden love for God can manifest itself when we study Torah or perform the *mitzvot*. We can also identify this hidden love in ourselves as we prepare for sleep. The Zohar says:

> I long and yearn for You like a man who craves the life of his soul, and when he is weak and exhausted he longs and yearns for his soul to revive in him; and also when he goes to sleep he longs and yearns for his soul to be restored to him when he awakens from his sleep. So do I long and yearn to draw the light of the blessed Endless One, the Life of true life, within me through occupation in the Torah when I awaken during the night from my sleep.[23]

Even when we are exhausted, the inner longing to be full of strength and vitality is itself a small part of our hidden love for God. And we can pray that the light of the Endless One will infuse our being not only if we awaken to study Torah, but even in our dreams.

We are drawn to the love of God, Hasidic teachings say, just as the flame of a candle is drawn upward. This is what pulls us toward prayer or meditation, or toward people who seem to have a spiritual life. This instinct sometimes flickers or disappears if it is not nourished. But the active life of prayer and *mitzvot* can help it burst into flame again.

Saying the *Shema* is like putting on a wedding ring. It takes us to the deep connection we have with God, whether or not we feel it at that moment. Just as Oneness (*Echad*) is not always recognized, so also with love (*ahavah*). Like a marriage, there are moments when the connection is very deeply felt. At other times, we work consciously to maintain the connection even though we don't feel it. But the wedding ring tells us it is still there. Just as our marriages are based on an agreement that has been inscribed in the *ketubah* (marriage contract), so our relationship to God is also a covenant that does not change even when our feelings fluctuate. We can imagine it as a rainbow—which also represents a covenant between God and humanity—arching over us as we say the *Shema*.

The committed, covenantal relationship of love is expressed during the day through actions. When we say the *Shema* at bedtime, however, we are not preparing ourselves for action or focusing on the *mitzvot* of the day. Rather, we are turning inward to connect with the deep, hidden love of God.[24] While the *Shema* of the daytime turns us toward our commitments on behalf of God—how we can bring Torah into the world as we go out through our doorposts and gates—the bedtime *Shema* asks us to be present to our inmost yearnings.

Imagine how we prepare the house for the night. We shut the doors, close the curtains on the windows, turn out the lights in the public rooms, and retire to the bedroom. We might touch the *mezuzah*s as we go through the house, thinking of the *Shema*. We say goodnight to the people of our household. Then we change out of our daytime clothing, wash off the dust of the day, and go to bed. One by one, these actions slowly direct us inward. Then, with the *Shema*, we follow the heart and soul in their inmost desires, to the ultimate love and comfort of God. Saying the *Shema* strengthens the *neshamah*, the soul. It infuses our spirit with love for God, and its sparks reach out, spinning a rainbow in our sky, arching over our *sukkah* of peace and into the world of dreams.

Movement and Meditation for the *Shema*

Traditionally, we cover our eyes with our right hand when saying the first line of the *Shema*. If you want to try an alternative to this, here is one:

1. Breathe a few times. As you inhale, make the sound "sh." As you exhale, quietly make the sound "ma."

2. Place your hands a few inches in front of your eyes with your fingertips touching so that your hands form a shield in front of your eyes. Say the first word of the prayer, *Shema*.

3. As you say *Yisrael*, slowly lift your hands, rotating them around each other in small circles, palms facing you, as you extend your arms higher.

4. Bring your hands down to the heart, criss-crossing them as if weaving a braid of energy. You may want to imagine colored strands, joining together in a soft white light at your heart. Say *Adonai Elohenu*. End with the right hand over the left at your heart. Think of the two names of God, *Adonai* and *Elohim*, becoming one.

5. With your hands on your heart, say *Adonai Echad*, extending the word *Echad*. Imagine Divine Light entering your body and extending outward in all four directions. Let your hands rest on your heart and sit quietly.

6. Imagine that everything in the room is lit from inside with a Divine Light. Open your eyes and see the light around you. In a whisper, say *Baruch shem kevod malchuto leolam va'ed.*

7. Close your eyes again, and say the first paragraph of the *Shema* (below), directing the loving energy in your heart and directing it to your Divine Source:

שְׁמַ**ע** יִשְׂרָאֵל, יהוה אֱלֹהֵינוּ, יהוה אֶחָ**ד**:
בָּרוּךְ שֵׁם כְּבוֹד מַלְכוּתוֹ לְעוֹלָם וָעֶד.

וְאָהַבְתָּ אֵת יהוה אֱלֹהֶיךָ,
בְּכָל־לְבָבְךָ, וּבְכָל־נַפְשְׁךָ, וּבְכָל־מְאֹדֶךָ.
וְהָיוּ הַדְּבָרִים הָאֵלֶּה, אֲשֶׁר אָנֹכִי מְצַוְּךָ הַיּוֹם,
עַל־לְבָבֶךָ:
וְשִׁנַּנְתָּם לְבָנֶיךָ,
וְדִבַּרְתָּ בָּם,
בְּשִׁבְתְּךָ בְּבֵיתֶךָ,
וּבְלֶכְתְּךָ בַדֶּרֶךְ,
וּבְשָׁכְבְּךָ, וּבְקוּמֶךָ:
וּקְשַׁרְתָּם לְאוֹת עַל־יָדֶךָ,
וְהָיוּ לְטֹטָפֹת בֵּין עֵינֶיךָ:
וּכְתַבְתָּם עַל־מְזֻזוֹת
בֵּיתֶךָ וּבִשְׁעָרֶיךָ:

Shema Yisrael Adonai Elohenu Adonai Echad.
Baruch shem kevod malchuto leolam va'ed.

Ve'ahavta et Adonai Elohecha,
bechol levavecha uvechol nafshecha, uvechol me'odecha.
Vehayu hadevarim ha'elleh asher Anochi mitzavecha hayom
al levavecha.
Veshinantam levanecha
vedibarta bam
beshivtecha bevaitecha
uvelechtecha vaderech
uveshochbecha uvekumecha.
Ukshartam le'ot al yadecha
vehayu letotafot bein einecha,
uchetavtam al mezuzot
baitecha uvisharecha.

Hear, O Israel, Adonai is our God, Adonai is One!
Blessed be the Name of the Glory of his Kingdom forever.

You shall love Adonai your God with all your heart,
and with all your soul, and with all your resources.
These words that I command you today
shall be upon your heart.
You shall teach them diligently to your children,
and speak of them
when you are sitting in your house,
when you are walking on the road,
and when you lie down, and when you rise up.
You shall bind them as a sign upon your hand,
and they will be as reminders between your eyes,
and you shall write them on the doorposts
of your house and on your gates.

יְבָרֶכְךָ יהוה וְיִשְׁמְרֶךָ:
יָאֵר יהוה פָּנָיו אֵלֶיךָ וִיחֻנֶּךָ:
יִשָּׂא יהוה פָּנָיו אֵלֶיךָ וְיָשֵׂם לְךָ שָׁלוֹם:

May God bless you and guard you.

May God make the Divine Face shine
on you and be gracious to you.

May God lift up the Divine Face toward
you and give you peace.

5

Bircat Cohanim: Mighty Ones of Blessing— The Gift of Gavriel

Master of the universe! I am Yours and my dreams are Yours. I have dreamed a dream and I do not know what it is. May it be Your Will, Lord my God and God of my ancestors, that all my dreams concerning myself and anyone of Israel be for good, whether dreams that I dreamed about others, or whether I dreamed about myself, or whether others dreamed about me. If they are good, strengthen and reinforce them, and may they be fulfilled in me and in them, like the dreams of Joseph the righteous. And if they require a remedy, heal them like Hezekiah, King of Judah, from his illness, like Miriam the prophetess from her *tzara'at* [skin affliction], like Naaman from his *tzara'at*, like the waters of Marah by Moses and like the waters of Jericho by Elisha. As You have changed the curse of the wicked Balaam from a curse to a blessing, so may You change all my dreams concerning myself and all Israel to good. Guard me, be gracious to me, and favor me.

—Prayer for dreams, from a traditional prayerbook

The Priestly Blessing, sometimes known as the Threefold Blessing, appears in most versions of the Bedtime Prayers. This may seem strange at first—what is this blessing doing in a private and personal ritual? The original context of the blessing was the services in the Holy Temple, and now it is the public synagogue service, when *cohanim* (priests; historically descendants of the first High Priest, Aaron) bless the entire congregation. Its most familiar form, "May the Lord bless and guard you," clearly indicates that one person should be blessing another, but in the Bedtime Prayers we seem to be blessing ourselves. Yet the appearance of this blessing in the bedtime *Shema* holds profound implications. It is a message to us about the meaning of blessing, and about deepening our connection to God.

Before we discuss this, however, let's review some basic information about the Priestly Blessing:

- ☐ In traditional synagogues in America based on Ashkenazi (northern European) rituals, the ceremony of the Priestly Blessing occurs on holidays during the *Musaf* (Additional) service. In the Land of Israel, it is performed every day. In Reform synagogues, the rabbi or cantor often blesses the congregation with the same words.

- ☐ When the *cohanim* bless the congregation, they cover their heads and arms with prayer shawls and raise their hands with a specific formation of the fingers.

- ☐ As they are blessed, the people express awe by bowing their heads or covering their faces.

- ☐ The *cohanim* chant the blessing slowly in a distinctive melody used only at this time.

- ☐ During this chant, the congregation recites special prayers, including the prayer for dreams that heads this chapter.

- ☐ When the full ceremony is not performed, the *chazzan* (cantor) recites the Priestly Blessing at the appropriate place in the repetition of the *Amidah* (standing prayer).

- ☐ The text of the Priestly Blessing occurs also in the section of traditional morning blessings that thank God for the Torah.

☐ At home, Jewish parents customarily bless their children with the Priestly Blessing on Shabbat Eve before the Friday night meal.

To understand why this blessing was imported into the bedtime *Shema*, we will look more deeply at what a blessing is, and the unique "priestly" character of the blessing.

The Gift of Blessing in Our Lives

There are two kinds of blessing: one in which God is blessed, and one in which a person is blessed. The first is the traditional blessing that usually begins *Baruch ata Adonai, Elohenu Melech ha'olam*—Blessed are You, Lord our God, Ruler of the Universe." Such a blessing is both an affirmation of God's power and an appreciation of goodness in some aspect of life. We make such blessings over the performance of Torah commandments (the phrase *asher kideshanu bemitzvotav, vetzivanu,* "Who sanctified us with Divine commandments and commanded us," occurs in these). We also say them over such pleasures as food, drink, and pleasant fragrances and as a form of praise of God. Every section of the *Amidah*, which states our daily requests, ends with a blessing. Blessings are the signature of Jewish prayer.

The blessings directed toward God are frequently considered forms of thanksgiving. Mystically, they are vehicles for returning what we have received to its Source, like an offering that gives to God part of what we have received. The blessing completes the circuit, so to speak, of giving and receiving. The word *baruch* (blessed), which begins most Hebrew blessings, is related to the word *bricha*, which means a flowing stream, and to *baraka*, which appears in other Semitic languages and means Divine power. Both of these meanings emphasize that when we say *Baruch ata* (Blessed are You, Lord), we are affirming the powerful flow of energy from the ultimate Source that creates and sustains everything.

The second type of blessing is upon a person. When we bless a person, we are acting as a channel of Divine power, a channel of giving to a person who is ready to receive. For example, when we recite the traditional *Bircat Hamazon*, or Grace After Meals, we invoke blessings on those who have given us the meal:

> *Harachaman*, the Compassionate One! May God bless the master of this house and the mistress of this house, their children, and all that is theirs, just as our ancestors Abraham, Isaac, and Jacob were blessed in everything and from everything. Thus may God bless all of us together with a perfect blessing. Let us say Amen.

The Priestly Blessing is of this type. Usually, it is transmitted by specially designated people, the *cohanim*, but we see clearly from the Grace After Meals that any Jew may invoke a blessing from God and channel it toward another person.

A midrash says that God told Abraham that from the time of creation, God had personally blessed God's creatures, but beginning with Abraham, "the blessings are transferred to you. Whomever you wish to bless—bless!" This is the meaning of the verse, "And you shall be a blessing" (Genesis 12:2)[1].

But how does one person know how to bless another? What blessing should we ask God to give our children, or our friends? Rabbi Nosson Scherman writes that our ancestors possessed the ability to know how to bless. Their spiritual greatness came from *ruach hakodesh*, (the Holy Spirit) that enabled them to perceive the spiritual essence of each person, right to the core of his soul. Because they were not deceived by external appearance, they could bless each person according to his unique needs and potential .... "He blessed them, each in accordance with his own blessing did he bless them" (Genesis 49:28). In later generations, the *cohanim* did not always have *ruach hakodesh*, so God prescribed the Threefold Blessing in the precise order taught to Aaron and his sons.[2] This tells us that the Priestly Blessing focuses on the "spiritual essence" of a person, according to each person's needs and potential.

Blessings Increase Life's Goodness

Blessings have one additional and very important aspect. A blessing is considered a way that good things are increased. "Blessed are you, Lord, who blesses the years" seals a prayer for increase of our means of sustenance and growth. "Blessed are You, Lord, who heals the sick" ends the prayer for increase of healing. What makes it possible for the flow of goodness to increase is our saying the blessing, because we are opening ourselves to a direct relationship to God. If we imagine God's sustenance of the world as a stream flowing over a dam, the blessing opens the channels so that more water can flow. When we bless another person, we are also opening the channels, and asking the other person to be open to receive more.

Yet blessings are not really quantitative. They have to do with a perspective on life, with opening up one's vision. Telling children to "count" their blessings really means that they should recognize the goodness that is in their lives. You may remember being taught this by comparing yourself to others. If you wanted to complain about your cereal, you would be told to think of children (usually in some far off country) who didn't even have cereal. Later, you were probably taught to appreciate your privileges by comparing them with what you lacked when you were younger—when you couldn't stay up late, or when you weren't allowed to go out with friends.

In short, most of us have to learn about blessings. If we came into the world feeling blessed, we soon lost that sense of joy and gratitude. If we ever had an innate sense that Divine Fullness was flowing like a rushing stream into our lives, we learned early on to think of good things as scarce, expensive, or difficult to obtain. The spiritual lesson we need to learn is to reverse our perception—to recognize that blessings are coming all the time, even in disguise.

By the time we reach maturity, we have begun to see that. We grudgingly admit that the geometry teacher we hated actually taught us a lot, and that dealing with the obnoxious kids on the playground helped us learn to get along with people. But most of the time, we learn about such matters—and they are often major parts of our moral and spiritual development—only in hindsight. When some new challenge confronts us, we all too often react as though the universe has just slammed us with another disaster. We moan and groan, we fight it or procrastinate. We forget that these are the ways in which character is forged, and that the way we learn to address our challenges is much more important in the long run than the things that came very easily. These, in fact, are profound blessings.

Think of three or four circumstances of your life—these could be people who affected you or situations that you thought were obstacles, detriments, or even a curse. List them on a sheet of paper. Now spend a few moments reflecting: What did you do in response to those circumstances? How did you develop strategies? Have those responses and strategies helped you since? Have they taught you how to be a better person, or how not to be a worse one? Do you have talents or abilities that others do not have because of these experiences? Write down some of your ideas. In most cases, you will find that adversity can be seen as a disguised blessing. Usually we would not have chosen these for ourselves, but once we were given them, we found out how to survive and even excel in some ways precisely because of those adverse circumstances.

This is a clue to understanding blessing. The reality is that the Divine flow of love and goodness pours forth continuously. We, from our position in linear time, cannot see the ultimate outcome of events, so we judge some things as good (blessings) and others as evil (curses). When we feel put upon by the universe, we expend a great deal of energy in resentment, disappointment, and hopelessness. But if we could see more broadly and deeply, we would appreciate the potential for growth, development, evolution, "increase" of goodness, in every event. Instead of waiting for hindsight, we can accept the challenges that come to us and look forward to what we are being asked to learn.

The rabbis said that we can bless God for the evil as well as the good. In the world as it is now, we bless God for the good with a blessing, "Blessed is the one who is good and does good." We bless God for the evil with "Blessed is God the True Judge." Yet in messianic times we will bless God even for the evil that occurred in history with "Who is good and does good," because we will then possess that special perspective in which everything is for the good, and we will be able to find the good in everything.

Blessings, then, are for "increase." They are expressions of thanks for the "more" that God has given; they are prayers for the "more" we hope to receive. But most important, they are means of increasing and expanding our own consciousness, so that we can see the good and transmit that vision to others.

A Hasidic Story

Once a man came to his rabbi and said that he was tormented by the problem of evil: Everywhere, people suffered. Some people made money and then lost it, others had illness or grief. Why?

His rabbi replied that he could not answer the question, but he thought that if the man would visit Reb Zusya, one of the Hasidic masters, he might get an answer to his question. The man got directions and went immediately to Reb Zusya's house. Now Zusya lived in a very poor section of town, and his house was the least of any of them. When the man arrived, he saw that Zusya lived in a tiny cottage, badly in need of repair. Inside, he found a miniscule room with a table and chair, barely large enough for Zusya and his wife. Zusya himself looked thin and worn, but he welcomed his visitor and set before him a plate with a small piece of dry bread and a cup of water. The man realized that Zusya might be known for his devotion, but he was also one of the most impoverished individuals he had ever seen. Clearly, he was familiar with the sufferings of this world. The man's heart went out to him.

Zusya asked, "What brings you here?"

"I'm sorry to disturb you, Rebbe," said the man. "But I have been tormented by a question, and my rabbi sent me to you. Please tell me, what is the meaning of suffering?"

Zusya was quiet for a long time, thinking. Finally he looked up at the man and shrugged his shoulders. "I'm sorry. I don't know why your rabbi sent you to me. I don't have an answer. You see, I've never suffered."

The Threefold Blessing

With this perspective, let us look more closely at the Priestly Blessing. Traditional commentaries tell us that the first section, "May the Lord bless you and guard you," is a blessing for health, wealth, and security. The second section, "May the Lord make the Divine Face shine upon you and be gracious unto you," is a prayer for intellectual and spiritual growth because "shining" implies enlightenment. The third section, "May the Lord lift up the Divine Face to you and grant you peace," places a "seal" of peace on the rest of the blessing.[3]

Many traditional commentaries especially emphasize the blessing of peace. They link the emphasis on peace with Aaron, Moses' brother, who was the first High Priest. Aaron was a peacemaker par excellence. When, forty days after the Revelation on Sinai, some of the Israelites wanted to make a golden calf, he never acted harshly. He tried to procrastinate, and when the issue was forced, he became involved in the sin himself in order to placate and mollify the factions. When his sons died, he silently accepted their deaths. The midrash says that he worked hard to make peace between people who were quarreling. Rabbi Hillel advised, "Be of the disciples of Aaron, loving peace and pursuing peace, loving your fellow creatures and bringing them near to Torah.[4] Aaron emanated peace, and so the Priestly Blessing emphasizes his special quality.

The blessing of peace is so important because peace "seals" all other blessings. No matter what other forms of "increase" (i.e., blessing) God gives us, if we lack peace, they will be of no effect. If there is war in the world, it will undermine our good fortune—wealth, health, family, friends. Likewise, if we are not at peace within, the blessings that we may experience in the physical world will come to naught. To close our day with the Priestly Blessing's prayer for peace means that we are putting a seal around all that we have received during the day.[5]

Yet this approach slides over some of the most interesting facets of the blessing. We can read the first verse straightforwardly to say, "May the Lord increase [what you have] and guard you [so you can keep it]." But questions arise with the second verse: What does it mean that God's "face" shines on a person? What is "graciousness"? In the third verse, what does it mean that God "lifts up the Divine Face to you"? This is especially odd, given the statement in Exodus 33:23 that "My face may not be seen."

Blessings Encircle Us with Light

We can answer the questions by turning to two verses that the commentaries connect to the Priestly Blessing. These verses occur in a biblical book known as *Shir Hashirim* (Song of Songs, also known as Song of Solomon). Jewish mysticism understood this book, ostensibly a poem about the love between a man and a woman, as an expression of the love between God and the Jewish people. Rabbi Akiva regarded it as the deepest expression of our relationship to God.

The two verses are: "Behold! He (my Beloved) stands behind our wall, looking through the windows, peering through the lattices" (Song of Songs 2:9), and "Behold, it is the bed of Shlomo, sixty mighty ones around it, of the mighty ones of Israel; each with his sword on his thigh, because of the dread of the nights" (Song of Songs 3:7–8).

According to the midrash, the first verse portrays God as providentially watching over us, accompanying us with the Divine Presence even though hidden. God gazes upon us while the *cohanim*, standing shoulder to shoulder, chant the Priestly Blessing. The spaces between their shoulders represent God "looking through the windows." Their fingers form a specific group of spaces, which alludes to "peering through the lattices."[6] The Priestly Blessing is thus portrayed as a channel for God's blessing even in the hidden places of our lives. It also hints at the possibility that the Divine Voice may come through to us as we receive or speak the blessing. As Rabbi Elie Munk, a twentieth-century commentator, puts it, "The *Shekhinah* fills the spaces, as it were, between the fingers and hands of the *cohanim*, even as, long ago, it rested in the space between the two *Cherubim* upon the Holy Ark."[7]

The second verse imagines the king being carried in a litter in a royal procession, and describes the king's bed surrounded by armed guards. The commentators compare sixty mighty men around King Solomon's bed to the sixty letters of the Priestly Blessing. When we use these letters to recite the blessing as we go to bed, we are recreating our own processional into the wonders of the night.

The description of the bed in royal procession is a beautiful one. It hints at the idea, also mentioned in the midrash, that one's bedroom is like the Temple. On the most basic level, the bed serves the purpose of being fruitful and multiplying, just as the Temple brought blessings of increase to the whole land of Israel and the world. On the walls of the

Temple were golden trees, alluding to fertility and growth, the Torah as Tree of Life and, the mystics would add, the Kabbalistic Tree of Life.[8]

The image of the armed men with swords, however, seems an odd one for bedtime, however appropriate it might be for a royal procession. The rabbinic tradition interpreted the sword as power in Torah learning and impeccability of behavior. An alternative way of understanding the imagery of the swords appears in Rav Kook's interpretation of a Talmud saying by Rabbi Yitzchak: "The whole of one's *Kriat Shema al Mitah* [bedtime *Shema*] is as if one grasped a two-edged sword, as it says (Psalms 149:6), 'Let God be exalted on their lips and a two-edged sword in their hands'" (*Berachot* 5a). Rav Kook explains that we should not understand "sword" literally, but rather as a metaphor for our "sharp" faculties. When our intellectual powers are available to us, we have great strength available to make a stance against the powers of evil. We can consider things and make decisions. But the physical powers have a hard time by themselves. When we are asleep, and the intellectual powers are dormant, it is as if we have only a one-edged sword. The negative influences that can come upon us while we sleep can affect us even later when we awaken.

Enter the bedtime *Shema*, which counteracts the negative influences:

> So our sages have given over to us the secrets of *Kriat Shema al Mitah* for the inflowing of positive energy that comes because of it, for it penetrates even to the physical power in a person, and he acquires in himself by this means an impression of great holiness within the power of knowledge, until on his own he is inclined to make himself stand up against the negative powers. Thus the meaning of the metaphor is that, by means of *Kriat Shema al Mitah*, it is like grasping a two-edged sword, that on both the side of the mental and the side of the physical, one is strong against his enemies, strong on all sides.[9]

In other words, saying the *Shema al Mitah* creates such a powerful influx of positive energy that it is as if a physical sword had cut through darkness. So we can imagine these prayers cutting through the cords of negativity that bind us to the cares of the daytime world.

An even more radical interpretation is offered by a midrash that allegorizes the verse:

☐ "His bed," *mitato*, can be vocalized differently in Hebrew to read *matoto*, his tribes."

☐ *Shel Shlomo*, "of Solomon," can be rearranged as s*halom lo*, "the one to whom peace belongs," namely God.

☐ The sixty mighty ones of Israel around the bed can be "sixty myriads," the 600,000 Jewish souls described in the Torah as God's host.

☐ The "dread of the night" alludes to the first Passover, when the angel of death came through Egypt, but did not kill the Jews who had put lamb's blood on the doorpost.[10]

The phrase on this reading would say, "The tribes of the One to Whom peace belongs! Six hundred thousand souls, going with swords on their thighs, on the dread night of their liberation!" This radical rereading of the verse asks us to visualize that going to bed is like leaving Egypt! It suggests that sleep carries us into a journey where, like the ancient Israelites freed from slavery, we can reconnect with our essence and our destiny.

One further aspect of this verse is the implication of the number sixty in "sixty mighty ones." The Priestly Blessing itself has sixty words. The number of letters in each verse is 15, 20, and 25 respectively, to make the total of 60. This is the numerical value of the letter *samech*. In addition, the blessing is made up of 3, 5, and 7 Hebrew words, totalling 15, and *samech* is the fifteenth letter in the Hebrew alphabet. Thus the three verses represent a double arithmetical progression (like a procession!) leading to the *samech*.

Samech is written as a circle and mystically, it refers to the "Surrounding Light" of God. According to the *Tanya*, a classic of modern Jewish mysticism, God's light is said to be present in two forms—the "Filling of the Worlds," or revealed light, which constitutes all that we know, and the "Surrounding of the Worlds," or encompassing light, which is hidden and concealed, pervading all the worlds without being directly known.[11] The sixty letters of the blessing symbolize a hidden circle of light within and around you when you say the prayer. The letter *samech* is also connected to *semicha*, "ordination," which refers to the practice by which a rabbi transfers authority to a student—just as in ancient times when one priest ordained another, and they put their hands on a sacrificial animal as a way of making connection to it. In the Priestly Blessing, there is a potential transfer of spiritual power. The "mighty ones" around us, the circle of light, the priests blessing the people with God gazing at us in amazement through our arms and hands—these all are images of our being infused with spiritual potential.

Our true beauty, of course, is from the inside out—from the root of the soul. Rabbi Steve Robbins pointed to this when he noted how the parts of the blessing correspond to the ten *sefirot* (channels of energy) as the diagram below shows.[12] The *sefirot* in a human being are centers of energy that replicate God's manifestation in creation. They are usually portrayed as organized in three "pillars"—center, left, and right—in a balanced form. In the Priestly Blessing, each of the three verses has two verbs, corresponding to right- and left-side pillars. Each verse has the name of God, marking out three *sefirot* for the pillar down the center. *Malchut*, the lowest *sefirah*, is represented by the word *Shalom*, which is another name of God.

In this diagram, the *sefirot* are surrounded by sixty *samechs*, which remind us of the hidden Surrounding Light.

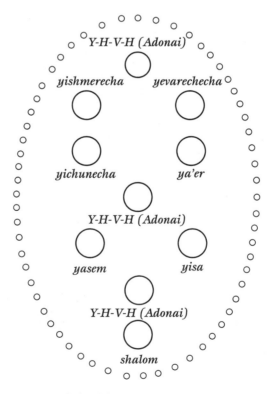

Since the structure of the blessing recapitulates the structure of the *sefirot*, the essential skeleton of the Kabbalistic interpretations of God, human beings, and the universe, we are being given a blessing connected to our soul's basic form. To put it in mystical terms: the Surrounding Light of *samech*, "60," is being connected to the Filling Light, the light manifest and visible in each of us. We are reciting a blessing that not only encircles us with light but also focuses on our radiant inner being.

The Blessing of Being Seen

Now we can return to the question of God's "Face," or the Countenance, as it is often translated. The *Tanya* says, "The term Countenance exemplifies the inner quality of the Supernal Will and true desire, in which God delights to dispense life from the realm of holiness to everyone who is near him."[13] As a human face can reveal what the person is thinking or wanting, so God's Face reveals the Divine intent. "May God make the Divine Face shine upon you" suggests that the blessing allows us to see God's true intent for us, which is to give life and vitality. With this blessing, we can experience ourselves as God sees us—as heirs of the royal heritage of King Solomon, as the people who were liberated from Egypt, and as gloriously woven of Divine qualities in the inner mystical structure of our souls.

Further, God sees with Divine love: God is "gracious to you." The Zohar says that there are two verses in Psalms that refer to the beauty of the original human being, Adam, namely: "And let the graciousness of the Lord our God be upon us" (Psalms 90:17) and "to behold the graciousness of the Lord" (Psalms 27:4). Adam's beauty at the time of his creation was so great that "the fleshy part of Adam's heel outshone the orb of the sun," and our ancestor Jacob also shared in that beauty.[14] When we say the blessing that the "graciousness" of God be upon us, we are assured of being seen in our original beauty.

"May God lift up the Divine Face to you and grant you peace." The blessing suggests that if we were truly rooted in our authentic being, God would "look up" to us. This reminds us that we were made in the Divine image, so we can be more Godly in our lives. When we are seen, it is like a mirror that helps us contemplate who we truly are and what our purpose in life is.

Being truly seen is a most powerful form of blessing. Many great rabbis have been said to be able to see the truth in others. People who met these special spiritual leaders reported that when they looked at you,

you felt as if you had been seen in your very soul. This seeing of a person's true essence is also a vision of his or her potential, the self that is not yet manifest in the world.

We all want to be seen in our simple essence of goodness. A child will come to a parent and say, "Just sit down and watch me while I color this page." We want this more than praise, more than any words. Yet being seen rarely happens in our lives. When it does, we are likely to become suddenly self-conscious.

Think of times that you have been seen. Perhaps you remember a moment when a friend, a lover, or a parent looked at you in a deep, knowing way. Your grandmother may have gazed at you with such love that it took you by surprise. Sometimes you have seen others in that way, too. Perhaps you struck up a friendship at summer camp and you both delighted in each other for those precious weeks. Perhaps a teacher or a doctor saw part of you that no one else had seen, and touched an inner truth.

In those moments, we become witnesses to each other's existence. When we are seen, we feel real. Just as the *Shema* represents our witness to the reality of God in our lives (the enlarged letters *ayin* and *dalet* spell "witness"), so we witness the reality, depth, and astounding complexity of other human beings. And, in the Priestly Blessing, God becomes our witness. Divine Light turns in our direction and illuminates us, seeing us in our inherent grace and beauty and sending us a gift of inner peace. Since *shalom*, peace, is related to *shalem*, completeness or perfection, to be granted peace is also to be granted a completion of one's being.

The Priestly Blessing thus not only seals what we have already received, but also reaches into a realm of potential, a realm of what we could be. It awakens the spark in each of us that is the Divine essence and intimates that the hidden light within can be revealed.

Becoming a Kingdom of Priests

The blessing asks us to visualize ourselves complete, in full bloom, as royalty. Because it is a Priestly Blessing, it also invites us to visualize ourselves as *cohanim*. Indeed, God told the Jewish people, "You shall be to me a kingdom of priests and a holy nation!" (Exodus 19:6).

What does it mean to be a priest? When we understand this, we will appreciate even more the connection between the Priestly Blessing and the *Shema al Mitah*, which is the doorway into the dream world.

The first "priest" mentioned in the Torah is actually not Jewish, but a figure much older than Abraham. In the Book of Genesis, a king of Salem named Melchizedek, whom tradition identifies as Shem, a son of Noah, is called "priest of the Most High God" (Genesis 14:18). He blessed Abraham and Abraham's God, implicitly transferring the power of blessing to Abraham. On this section, the Zohar teaches that the blessing of a priest creates the intersection between the upper and lower worlds through the special position of the hands:

> "And he was priest of God Most High," that is, one world ministers to the other. Priest refers to the right side [which in Kabbalah is the side of loving kindness], and Most High God to the upper world; hence a priest is required to bless the world. This lower world receives blessings when it is associated with a High Priest; hence there is a special force in the words "and he blessed him and said, Blessed is Abram to the Most High God." After this model it behooves the priest on earth to intertwine his fingers when blessing in the synagogue so that he may be linked with the right side and that the two worlds may be linked together.[15]

The power attributed to the Priestly Blessing goes back even before the beginnings of Judaism through Jacob, Isaac, and Abraham to Shem/Melchizedek, one of the survivors of the Flood.

Later, the *cohanim* have other special abilities. For example, they could diagnose the ancient skin affliction known as *tzara'at*. When a person appeared to have *tzara'at*, he or she had to go to the *cohain* to determine whether in fact the problem was this particular skin affliction, in which case the *cohain* would prescribe and oversee the required procedure (see Leviticus 13). A priest could not "heal" the *tzara'at*, but he could be a channel through which an appropriate correction could take place. The *cohain* lived by stricter laws—particularly having to do with food, death, and marriage—that created greater personal purity in his life. This, ideally, would make it possible for him to have a clear channel through which he could give the appropriate "diagnosis" and blessing. Perhaps not every *cohain* was equally able to do this, but the practices of the priesthood were intended to create a refinement and impeccability of behavior that would point him in that direction.

Another feature of the priesthood was a special function of the *Cohain Gadol* (the High Priest). He wore a breastplate, known as the *choshen*, a piece of woven fabric studded with gems engraved with holy letters that was folded so as to make a secret inner compartment. Inside this compartment was a set of objects called the *urim v'tummim* (probably best translated as "lights and perfections"). When a leader of the people, usually a king, had a question concerning the fate of the nation, he could bring the question to the *Cohain Gadol*. Tradition has it that a light inside the breastplate illuminated the letters—according to the Kabbalists, 72 letters—engraved on the external gems, revealing the answer to the question. Recent scholarship suggests that the stones inside the breastplate indeed reflected light and in some unusual way provided an authentication to what the priest received through a prophetic spirit.

Over time, this usage declined, and there was no *urim v'tummim* in the Second Temple. The Levites became teachers to the whole people rather than guardians of a secret knowledge. Nevertheless, it seems that part of the original priestly function was to be a channel for the interpretation of oracles.[16]

The priest blessed, diagnosed, and answered questions. He could do these things because he could see the true nature of reality: A blessing evokes the hidden goodness in a person. A diagnosis identifies the correct root of disease. Answers to questions of national importance were the core of prophecy. All these came from the inner being, the glowing heart, mediated by the special instruments of the *choshen* and *urim v'tummim*.

All the more significant, then, that the prayer for dreams at the beginning of this chapter is recited in an undertone during the Priestly Blessing in synagogue.[17] Dreams, too, are connected to the essence of one's being. It is no accident that the prayer compares the "healing" of dreams to the healing of a *tzara'at*. In ancient times, a person could go to a *cohain* with a troubling dream. Thus the midrash says of the Priestly Blessing, "If someone, in a dream, beholds a drawn sword pointed at his throat ... let him rise up in the morning and go to the house of God ... and let him hear there the blessing of the Priests, which will cancel his evil dream."[18] The recital of the blessing before one goes to sleep can help achieve the same effect in advance.

Now we can understand: The Priestly Blessing is intended to connect us to a power that heals us at a deeper level than our conscious, rational mind. It asks us to enter into Divine consciousness, where we see goodness and we become channels for goodness. This is the essence of the priestly calling. This is why the Zohar said that when the priests intertwine their fingers, they link the worlds. And the Jewish people, as a kingdom of priests, are the larger manifestation of that calling. When we say the Priestly Blessing, we are affirming that we are vessels of the Divine.

All the more appropriate, then, to recite the blessing at bedtime, when we are about to end our conscious efforts to control our world and enter the radically different world of sleep and dreams. The Priestly Blessing connects us to our highest selves, to our Divine image, and to the transcendent Light of God. With this blessing, we allow ourselves to be present to states of consciousness that are beyond the boundaries of spacetime. And we take with us into that expanded space a deep awareness of light, goodness, and peace.

Here is a meditation that you can use with your own recital of the Threefold Blessing.

Urim and Tummim *Meditation*

Sit on the edge of your bed, or lie down if you prefer. Close your eyes and breathe deeply, in and out. Be aware of the safety and comfort of your bed, surrounded by your sukkah *of peace.*

As you inwardly imagine yourself in your room, notice that on the wall, glass doors appear. See them slide open, leading down a hallway lit by the soft light of the moon, to a museum of Jewish treasures.

You walk through an archway that leads into a room of ancient Temple treasures. Gold and silver and copper glitter from each glass case, but what attracts you most deeply is straight ahead, at the end of the room, a series of glass cases in which the garments of the High Priests have been miraculously preserved. In each glass case hangs a magnificent robe, each slightly different, and on each one is a breastplate woven with beautiful threads and gems. You know that this contained the Urim *and* Tummim, *the stones worn by the High Priest in each generation to give him Divine guidance.*

You walk around the glass cases and you see one robe that especially attracts you. Look at the intricately woven fabric of the robe, its colors and patterns, the bells and pomegranates that decorate the hem. The breastplate is mesmerizing with its sacred stones and engraved letters, its mysterious compartments. As you gaze at it, the stones begin to glow with a radiant light.

Soon, you notice that the door of the glass case is ajar. It swings open gently, inviting you to try on the robe and breastplate. You wrap the robe around yourself and place the breastplate on your chest. What is it like to wear sacred clothing? Does it help you feel more connected to your Divine Source? Does it awaken any desire to reach toward more holiness in your life?

You are guided by an inner directive toward a room that represents the sanctuary of the ancient Temple. As you walk, notice if the way you carry yourself is different. Do you take your steps in a different manner? How in your own life would you walk if you were dressed in these clothes?

A chair awaits you in the sanctuary. It feels comfortable, and you sit for a few moments, becoming more aware of the breastplate at your heart. Is it heavy or light? The twelve stones begin to radiate with light, and you feel them moving from their place. Three of them rise from the breastplate and settle themselves on top of your head, forming a tiny crown. How do they feel? Do any colors emanate from them?

The remainder of the stones, one by one, place themselves on your body in the configuration of the remaining nine sefirot. One stone moves to the right temple, one to the left. One places itself at the right shoulder, one at the left. Another stays at the heart. One moves to the right hip, one to the left, one to the pubic bone. The last stone appears at the feet. Notice whether you see a particular kind of stone or a specific color at any of the locations. Feel the radiant energy that each one emanates, and feel it infuse your spirit with Divine connection.

Bask in the gift of the energy of the stones for a moment. Then you will say the blessing three times. (The blessing is given in full at the end of the chapter; here, the blessing is written along with the movement.)

Yevarechecha Adonai veyish-merecha.
May God bless you and guard you.

1. Touch the crown of your head with the fingers of both hands.

Move your hands out beyond your temples and curve them in toward your neck. Clasp your hands together in front of your heart. Hold for a moment.

Ya'er Adonai panav eilecha vichuneka.
May God make the Divine Face shine on you and be gracious to you.

2. Move your hands out toward your shoulders, then curve them inward toward your heart.

Clasp them together in front of your heart, and hold again.

Yisa Adonai panav eilecha,
May the Lord lift up the Divine Face
toward you

3. Move your hands out and down past
your hips, curving them in at your navel.

Clasp your hands there and hold.

...veyasem lecha,
And give you

4. As if you are washing yourself with
energy, move your hands and arms forward, up, and around, making a circle
from your navel, out in front of your chest,
and up above your head. Bring your hands
down, scanning the front of your body.

shalom.
Peace.

5. Let your hands relax at your sides. Feel the energy in and around you.

6. Repeat the blessing and the movement.

7. If you have been sitting, lie down. Say the blessing one more time,
repeating the movement.

Now see the stones back at their original places on the breastplate. Are you aware of any blessings you have been given? Is there a blessing you would like to give yourself now? Is there a blessing you would like to give someone else? Now is the time to do it, in your own words.

See yourself rising now, leaving the sanctuary and returning to the treasure room with the glass cases. Return the robe and breastplate to their place. The glass case closes and, as you walk out of the room and the museum, it fades away behind you. The moonlit path in front of you guides you right to your bed, where you are almost ready for sacred sleep.

יְבָרֶכְךָ יהוה וְיִשְׁמְרֶךָ:

יָאֵר יהוה פָּנָיו אֵלֶיךָ וִיחֻנֶּךָּ:

יִשָּׂא יהוה פָּנָיו אֵלֶיךָ וְיָשֵׂם לְךָ שָׁלוֹם:

Yevarechecha Adonai veyishmerecha.

Ya'er Adonai panav eilecha vichuneka.

Yisa Adonai panav eilecha veyasem lecha shalom.

May God bless you and guard you.

May God make the Divine Face shine
on you and be gracious to you.

May God lift up the Divine Face toward
you and give you peace.

בָּרוּךְ אַתָּה יהוה אֱלֹהֵינוּ מֶלֶךְ הָעוֹלָם,

הַמַּפִּיל חֶבְלֵי שֵׁנָה עַל עֵינָי,

וּתְנוּמָה עַל עַפְעַפָּי.

וִיהִי רָצוֹן מִלְּפָנֶיךָ

יהוה אֱלֹהַי וֵאלֹהֵי אֲבוֹתַי,

שֶׁתַּשְׁכִּיבֵנִי לְשָׁלוֹם וְתַעֲמִידֵנִי לְשָׁלוֹם.

וְאַל יְבַהֲלוּנִי רַעְיוֹנַי,

וַחֲלוֹמוֹת רָעִים, וְהַרְהוֹרִים רָעִים.

וּתְהֵא מִטָּתִי שְׁלֵמָה לְפָנֶיךָ,

וְהָאֵר עֵינַי פֶּן אִישַׁן הַמָּוֶת.

כִּי אַתָּה הַמֵּאִיר לְאִישׁוֹן בַּת עָיִן.

בָּרוּךְ אַתָּה יהוה,

הַמֵּאִיר לָעוֹלָם כֻּלּוֹ בִּכְבוֹדוֹ.

Blessed are You, Adonai our God, Ruler of the Universe,
Who casts the bonds of sleep on my eyes
and slumber on my eyelids.
May it be Your Will,
Adonai my God and God of my ancestors,
that You lay me down in peace and raise me up to peace.
May my ideas, bad dreams
or evil fantasies not trouble us.
May my bed be complete before You,
And may You illuminate my eyes, lest sleep be death.
For You are the Illuminator of the pupil of the eye.
Blessed are You, Adonai,
Who illumines the whole world with the Divine Glory.

6

Hamapil: Seeing in the Dark— The Gift of Uriel

AHAB TOLD JEZEBEL all that Elijah had done and how he had put all the prophets [of Baal] to death with the sword. Jezebel then sent a messenger to Elijah saying, "The gods do the same to me and more, unless by this time tomorrow I have taken your life as you took theirs." He was afraid and fled for his life.

When he reached Beersheba in Judah, he left his servant there and went a day's journey into the wilderness. He came upon a broom-bush and sat down under it and prayed for death .... He lay down under the bush and, while he slept, an angel touched him and said, "Rise and eat." He looked, and there at his head was a cake baked on hot stones and a pitcher of water. He ate and drank and lay down again. The angel of the Lord came again and touched him a second time, saying, "Rise and eat; the journey is too much for you." He rose and ate and drank and, sustained by this food, he went on for forty days and forty nights to Horeb, the mount of God. He entered a cave and there he spent the night.

> Suddenly the word of the Lord came to him. "Why are you here, Elijah?" "Because of my great zeal for the Lord God of Hosts," he said. "The people Israel have forsaken Your covenant.... I alone am left, and they seek to take my life." The answer came, "Go and stand on the mount before the Lord." For the Lord was passing by: A great and strong wind came rending mountains and shattering rocks before him, but the Lord was not in the wind; and after the wind there was an earthquake, but the Lord was not in the earthquake; and after the earthquake fire, but the Lord was not in the fire; and after the fire a still small voice.
>
> —2 Kings 19:1–13

Praying for Light

After all our preparation for sleep, the final prayer at bedtime is the *Hamapil*, "Who casts the bonds of sleep on my eyes." Besides the *Shema*, the *Hamapil* is the only other "required" prayer in the bedtime service. We have seen how the *Shema*, with its focus on listening to God and on unity and love, expresses fundamental aspects of the Jewish view of God. The *Hamapil* summarizes the intent of the other Bedtime Prayers and then adds a unique and beautiful prayer for light— the light to see beyond the realities of the mundane world. This is the light of revelation, quietly emerging in the darkness, like the still small voice that Elijah heard on the mountain.

Probably no regular prayer has received so little commentary. What we say here is constructed of fragments garnered from many different places, none of which is absolutely authoritative. We offer it in hope that these comments will illuminate your night as they have ours.

There are really five parts to the *Hamapil*, which we will take in order.

☐ *Baruch ata Adonai, Elohenu melech haolam, Hamapil chevlei shena al einai utenumah al afapai.* "Blessed are You .... Who casts the bonds of sleep on my eyes and slumber on my eyelids." This is a mirror of one of the morning blessings, which says "Blessed are You ... who removes sleep from my eyes and slumber from my eyelids." It thanks God for the gift of sleep, as we thank God in the morning for the gift of waking up.

☐ *Vihi ratzon milfanecha, Adonai Elohai vElohei Avotai, shetashkivenu leshalom, veta'amidenu leshalom.* "May it be Your Will, *Adonai* my God and God of my ancestors, that you lay us down in peace and raise us up to peace." Here we have an echo of the *Hashkivenu*, probably from a time before that prayer itself was imported as a regular part of the bedtime *Shema*. In other words, the composer of the *Hamapil* inserted a hint of the Evening Prayer and asked for a blessing of peace on the individual.

☐ *Ve'al yevahaluni rayonai, vacholomot ra'im, veharhorim ra'im.* "May my ideas, bad dreams or evil fantasies not trouble me." Here the prayer asks for spiritual protection of the faculties of thought and imagination, just as the *Hashkivenu* asked for protection from other kinds of harm. Importantly, this section acknowledges the direct connection of this prayer to dreams.

☐ *Utehei mitati shlema lifanecha.* "May my bed be complete [or "perfect"] before You." This can have several meanings. One commentary suggests the interpretation that we should pray that our children and grandchildren should all be connected to God. On this line of thought, "bed" is a euphemism for sexual relations. This seems quite appropriate. Judaism has no other regular prayers that ask for blessings over our sexual relations, yet the mystical texts repeatedly refer to the connection between chaste sexual relations and "keeping the covenant" (the primary symbol of the covenant being, for males, circumcision). If we are engaging in intimate relations, the *Hamapil* prayer can be said with the intention of attuning our words and acts to God's Will. Reflecting on the depth and quality of our sexual relations can certainly be an aspect of a prayer said in bed.

More generally, however, the phrase "may my bed be complete" suggests the wholeness of intent involved in making sleep a holy act. As we suggested in the section on the Priestly Blessing, the actual place where we lie can be like a temple of the Divine. Hasidic teaching recommends that when we make our beds, we should have holy thoughts so that our pillows will be like Jacob's holy "altar" of twelve stones under his head.[1] An "altar" is a physical place designed with spiritual intent, to express a desire to connect to God. To ask that "my bed be complete" is to request that our intent be accepted, that all the preparations we make be as if we had actually built a temple and an altar to God.

☐ *Veha'er einai pen ishan hamavet, ki ata hameir le'ishon bat ayin. Baruch ata, Adonai, hameir la'olam kulo bichevodo.* "And enlighten my eyes lest sleep be death, for You are the illuminator in sleep of the pupil of the eye. Blessed are You, *Adonai*, who illuminates the whole world with the Divine Glory." This is a unique and rather peculiar set of phrases. "Enlighten my eyes"—but we have just thanked God for closing our eyes and putting slumber on our eyelids. "You are the illuminator of the pupil of the eye"—what does this expression mean here? "You illuminate the whole world"—at night?

> It is written, The Lord is One and His Name is One (Zechariah 14:9) ... and the revealed world is linked with the concealed.
>
> So was the appearance of the brightness round about; this was the appearance of the likeness of the Glory of the Lord (Ezekiel 1:28).
>
> "The appearance of the brightness round about," namely, the radiance that is hidden in the pupil of the eye, becomes "the appearance of the likeness of the Glory of the Lord."
>
> —Zohar

The prayer is clearly saying something about our eyes and our inner vision. Normally—that is, in daytime—the eye registers images when light enters through the pupil and strikes the retina in a way that is usually compared to light contacting photographic film. The information captured on the retina is decoded by the brain into images of the world we see. But when we are asleep, with eyelids tightly shut ("bonds of sleep cast on our eyes"), what is the source of the images that our mind "sees" in dreams? The *Hamapil* prayer is telling us that God is the source. God enlightens the eyes in the dark, illuminating the pupil of the eye even when no light enters from outside. The prayer is speaking of the inner eye, the ability to see that which is illuminated in dreams.

Such illumination is entirely dependent, as Rabbi Moshe Chaim Luzzatto says, on Divine decree:

> The information is revealed to the soul [*neshamah*] by one of God's servants, of whatever type it may be. It is then transmitted down to *nefesh* [soul] and visualized by the imagination, either clearly or obscurely, as decreed by the Highest Wisdom. Regarding such dreams, the Scriptures say, "In a dream, in a vision of the night ... [God] opens the ears of a person" (Job 33:15–16).[2]

There is an inner seeing, and it is something that comes from God. It is not an aspect of personality to be controlled by the ego—indeed, Jewish tradition indicates we should almost always be receptive rather than controlling in our dreams.[3] By saying a blessing, by uttering *Baruch ata*, ... we acknowledge the Higher Source of our dreams. The *Hamapil*, is a prayer of true surrender to the Divine. We are saying, "You, God, are the One who gives illumination—to me and to the whole world. Revelation in dreams is possible."

The end of the prayer mentions God illuminating the whole world with Divine Glory. This can mean the revelation of God that is in everything, especially in the starry night. But "glory" also sometimes refers, in mystical texts, to the human soul. We can imagine that in the night, as souls ascend to *Gan Eden*, they light up the darkness like the stars and constellations. On the personal level we are saying, if it be Your Will, the Glory that is my soul will be a channel for the Divine Light.

Judaism's Dreaming Tradition

The enlightenment of the eyes referred to in the *Hamapil* prayer comes from the light that illumines the soul. We receive that light through dreaming. The Jewish sages recognized the potential of dreaming, and we find in many classic texts strong views about dreaming and dream interpretation. To appreciate this, we want first to come to a basic understanding of what dreams are. Because our culture has minimized or compartmentalized the significance of dreams, it is important to attune our minds to the possibility of dream information.

Even a superficial reading of the Bible shows that dreams were regarded as significant in ancient Israelite times. The most important dreams were regarded as prophetic. An example is the famous prophecy of the future Jewish nation that was given to Abraham when he was seventy years old. When we read it in the Torah, we often forget that this was a great dream:

> And it happened, as the sun was about to set, a deep sleep fell upon Abram and behold, a dread, great darkness fell upon him. And [God] said to Abram, "Know with certainty that your offspring shall be aliens in a land not their own, they will serve them, and they will oppress them four hundred years. But also the nation that they shall serve, I will judge, and afterward they shall leave with great wealth. As for you—you shall come to your ancestors in peace; you shall be buried in a good old age. And the fourth generation will return here, for the iniquity of the Amorite shall not yet be full until then."
>
> —Genesis 15:12–16

Joseph, the link between the patriarchs and the later era of the tribes, was known as both a "dreamer" and an interpreter of dreams in Pharaoh's court. In addition, the early traditions record other dream-like experiences, generally called visions, which occurred when the individuals were awake. The prophets, who were trained in accessing unusual states of consciousness, nurtured Judaism through the entire period of the judges and kings (ca. 1200–586 B.C.E.).

Visions and dreams played a less central role after the Babylonian exile. Prophets continued, though in lesser roles, even down to the Hellenistic period (beginning in 333 B.C.E.), and the apocalyptic literature composed after the close of the biblical canon also relied on some kind of visionary tradition. But Torah study had almost completely replaced the direct access of information through altered states of consciousness. Nevertheless, the sages of the Babylonian Talmud (ca. 600 C.E.) still had a healthy respect for dreams, and that positive attitude continued in the mystical traditions.

The primary discussions of dreams in the Talmud appear in its first volume, *Berachot*, as a digression from a line of discussion about the varieties of blessings that can be said. Two characteristics stand out in this discussion: First, a dream is a gift. Perhaps that is why the discussion is included in "blessings." It is considered a source of healing, and the Talmud quotes Isaiah 38:16 on this point: "You caused me to dream and made me live" (*Berachot* 57b). Second, dreams have prophetic qualities; they are "one-sixtieth of prophecy."

Yet the gift of the dream often comes in disguise. It has to be interpreted: "A dream that is not interpreted is like a letter that is not read" (*Berachot* 55a). Even more importantly, it has to be interpreted for the good because "All dreams follow the mouth" (*Berachot* 55b), the mouth meaning the interpretation given to the dream. The proof text is from the Torah itself: "It came to pass; as he interpreted it, so it was" (Genesis 41:13).

A ritual developed in ancient times—which some still practice—for a person who had a troubling dream. He was to go to three people (a "dream court") and have it interpreted, specifically to "have a good turn given to it." He would tell them the dream, and they would say the following formula:

> Good it is and good may it be.
> May the Compassionate One turn it to good.
> Seven times may it be decreed upon you from heaven that it should be good, and may it be good.

The group would then recite nine biblical verses, three containing the word "turn," three with "redeem," and three with "peace" (*Berachot* 55b).

As for the prophetic quality of dreaming, the rabbis of the Talmud said that no dream has every element fulfilled, and all dreams have some nonsense within them (*Berachot* 55a). But on the other hand, one should hold out hope for the fulfillment of a good dream for twenty-two years, for that is how long Joseph had to wait. Rabbi Yochanan taught that three kinds of dreams are fulfilled: early morning dreams; dreams that friends have about each other; and a dream that is interpreted inside the dream. Others add that we can expect a repeated dream to be fulfilled.[4]

The Talmud also lists good dream omens, such as:

> If one sees a well, he will behold peace. A river, a kettle, and a bird are omens of peace.
> If one sees a reed, he may hope for wisdom.
> If one dreams that he eats an ox, he will become rich.
> If one dreams he is gored by an ox, his sons will contend for status in Torah study.

> If one dreams he is kicked by an ox, he will go on a long journey.
>
> If one dreams of a cat, it depends on what the cat is called in the place he is from—it means either a beautiful song will be composed for him, or there will be a change for the worse.
>
> If one dreams of Ishmael, Abraham's son, his prayer will be heard—but only if it is Ishmael, not an ordinary Arab.
>
> If one dreams of a dead person in the house, it is a dream of peace. If the dead person eats or drinks something in the house, it's a good sign.
>
> —*Berachot* 56b–57a, b

While some of these might seem humorous to us, it is important to note that most of the omens—especially those that we might expect to be frightening—are interpreted in a positive way. Very few have a negative connotation.

Second, many of the interpretations depend on a play on words, like the meaning of a dream of a cat depending on what the cat is called in a particular dialect; similarly with the words for river, kettle, and bird. This tells us an important fact, one that Freud made a cornerstone of his dream interpretation: Dreams are full of metaphor and symbol. They speak a language that can be interpreted only if we grasp the unique language of the dream. This concept tells us that "dream books" have a limited usefulness because they assume a universal dream language that does not exist. The Talmud's interpretation of ox dreams would not be appropriate for a dream of an ox in the twenty-first century. On the other hand, we have found some ways to break the code of contemporary dreams, which we will discuss later in this chapter.

The Jewish approach is quite different from the modern psychological approach that emphasizes the emotional quality of dreams and the idea that one's everyday experiences or childhood traumas are the main source of dreams. The sages implicitly recognize that view by telling a story about a Roman official who asked a rabbi to tell him what he would dream that night. The sage "prophesied" that he would be tormented. The Roman thought about it all day, and sure enough, he dreamed about it that night. Clearly, this is told to poke fun at someone who took dreams too lightly. But it also illustrates the view that if you go into the world of sleep with anxiety, it will disturb your dreaming.

The Talmud also tells a lengthy story about a person who interpreted dreams for money. The more you paid him, the better interpretation you received. Yet the outcome did follow the interpretation, so that even some rabbis were taken in by the man.

The Talmud's ideas about dreaming are amplified in later literature such as the Zohar, which recognizes the importance of positive interpretations of dreams.

> A man should not tell his dream save to a friend .... Joseph communicated his dream to his brothers, and they caused its fulfillment to be delayed for twenty-two years .... He begged his brothers to listen to him and insisted on telling them his dream which, had they given it another meaning, would have been fulfilled accordingly. But they said to him: "Shall you indeed reign over us? Or shall you have dominion over us?" And with these words they sealed their own doom.[5]

Similarly, the Zohar says, "When a man has had a dream, he should unburden himself of it before men who are his friends so that they should express to him their good wishes and give utterance to words of good omen."[6] We should cherish our good dreams:

> One ought to remember a good dream because, although there is no forgetfulness before the Holy One, yet if the man forgets the dream he will also be forgotten. A dream that is not remembered might as well not have been dreamt, and therefore a dream forgotten and gone from mind is never fulfilled. Joseph therefore kept his dream fresh in his memory, never forgetting it, so that it should come true, and he was constantly waiting for its fulfillment.[7]

The eighteenth-century Hasidic master Rabbi Schneur Zalman of Liadi taught that having good, insightful dreams is connected to our activities and efforts while awake. If we have devoted ourselves to Torah study and prayer, our souls ascend at night and receive new understandings of Torah. On the other hand, if we have been preoccupied with trivia during the day, dreams can also effectively mock us with trivial dreams as well.[8]

The Zohar and later mystics followed the Talmud in recognizing the potential for prophecy in dreams:

> Nothing happens in the world but what is made known in advance either by means of a dream or by means of a proclamation. Before any event comes to pass in the world it is announced in heaven, whence it is broadcast to the world. So

Scripture says, "For the Lord God will do nothing, but he reveals his counsels to his servants the prophets" (Amos 3:7) .... When prophets were no more, their place was taken by the sages, ... and in the absence of sages things to come are revealed in dreams; and if not in dreams, through the medium of the birds of heaven.[9]

Further, there are different levels of dreaming. Each person has his or her own levels of dreaming: "God communicates to each man by means of dreams of the degree and shade of color conformable to the degree and shade of color of the man himself."[10] From a more general perspective, the Zohar says that the passage "And God spoke to him in visions of the night" (Genesis 46:2) actually refers to six levels of vision. These vary in clarity and interpretability.[11] From this we can see that dreams were still taken very seriously, although one had to have considerable expertise to know a dream from a vision, and to know how to interpret either one.

In later mysticism we know that certain individuals relied a great deal on dreams. Joseph Caro, the great legal scholar who compiled the Code of Jewish Law, was visited in dreams by a teacher who helped him resolve *halakhic* problems. The Baal Shem Tov apparently was inspired by visions and dreams, and he could induce dream-like states in his followers so that they could accompany him on his visionary journeys. Certainly, the cognitive side of Torah study counted for more in everyday life, but in times of crisis dreamers and visionaries were still important features of Jewish life until rationalism triumphed in major nineteenth-century European Jewish communities. Even today, the masters of practical Kabbalah seek resolutions to problems in what is called a "Revelation of Elijah" (*gilui Eliyahu*), which is usually a dream that occurs after forty days of fasting and ceremonial preparations.[12]

Dreaming as a Way of Seeing

That we would all be dreamers and visionaries has actually been part of the messianic "dream" of Judaism: "I will pour out my spirit on all flesh, and your sons and daughters shall prophesy, your old men shall dream dreams, your young men shall see visions...." (Joel 3:1ff).

"When God returns the captivity of Zion, we will be like dreamers!" (Psalm 126). Does this mean we should all be in training to be prophets like those of biblical times? Probably not. What we really want is to get in touch with our own "still, small voice," as Elijah experienced in his vision. Just as Elijah found the words he needed to hear only after the static of wind and earthquake and fire had passed, so we want to hear the Divine truth that is meant for us.

If we understand the relationship between prophecy and dreaming, we can understand better how to hear that voice. Let's first become clear about what is meant by "prophecy." Prophets in ancient times were individuals who saw clearly. By their natural gifts or through training, they had subdued their bodies so that physical experiences did not interfere with receiving information beyond the senses. Through meditative techniques, they could transcend the ordinary mind. Their visions came without the many veils that obscure what is really going on at deeper levels. In such states, it is possible that prophets might transcend ordinary space and time and glimpse the future. Even most prophets, however, saw the future indirectly, through images and symbolic language.

Today, the word "prophecy" may refer to different things, depending on context. It can mean the highest levels of vision, where space-time is transcended and the potential of the future is visible, which is what the biblical prophets experienced. Or the word can be used for any of the variants of prophetic, clairvoyant, telepathic, and highly intuitive experiences in which a person seems to receive information from beyond the normal senses. What is common to all these is an ability to "see" more clearly. What differs is the range—how far the experience extends in space or time—and the modality—whether one sees visions or hears voices, for example.

Judaism preserved in its holy texts records of major prophecy, the visions and auditions that revealed important truths about the Jewish people and their relationship to God at critical points in history. Frequently, they warned the people of potential disasters; sometimes they offered hope for a great redemption. In certain circumstances, prophets revealed personal truths to individuals, as the prophet Nathan did for King David and the woman of Endor did for King Saul. The prophetic books chosen by the sages to become part of the Bible were regarded as having import far beyond their own time and place.

The kind of "prophecy" that is accessible through dreaming can also be a clear seeing, but it is more like the seeing discussed in Chapter 5, where you are seen so deeply that you feel as if you had been seen in your very soul. This seeing of a person's true essence is also a vision of his or her potential, the self that is not yet manifest in the world. This can become manifest in dreams because, as Rabbi Schneur Zalman of Liadi taught, dreams come from a higher world.[13] Moreover, the not-yet-manifest self is often larger than the personal self. The dream can reveal how your influence extends beyond the ordinary self, how you work with others, and how you are part of a larger collective. In this way, the dream world can draw forth our deepest truth, our not-yet-manifest potential.

Dreaming has other similarities to prophecy. The ancient prophets were able to nullify their bodies and ordinary minds; in sleep, our voluntary muscles shut down and our linear minds turn off. At that time, we are open to information normally not available to us. Prophecies were often coded in symbols; so are dreams. Both have to be deciphered. Moreover, as many writers have noted, the dream world is the fountain of imagination and an important source of creativity. Dreams allow us to imagine new possibilities, just as prophecy helped people anticipate the unexpected.

But dreams do not merely help us become more creative. They bring forth our spiritual selves. The only obstacles to that revelation are ones we create, through emotional attachments that keep our souls busy with tangled energy, and through mental projections that color our dream interpretations with fear. If we can clear ourselves, then we can let sleep be our opportunity to return to the dream-weave of the *Shekhinah* and to bring down through the worlds what God wants to give us. With greater access to our dreams, we can remember who we are meant to be.

The way our modern lives are structured, we know only half of ourselves—the waking half. When we begin to allow dreaming to have its proper place in our lives, we discover another part. As individuals and as part of the larger collective, we need to get in touch with that other, long suppressed and derided part of ourselves. How do we do this? For that, we will now synthesize what we know from Jewish tradition and our own experience.

Understanding the Process of Dreaming[14]

Dreams do not usually deliver their messages directly. Luzzatto taught that one of God's "servants" (such as an angel) delivers a message that is then transmitted down to the *nefesh* where it is visualized by the imagination. Sometimes you may have a very clear message such as an "oracular" dream, which is a verbal instruction or specific verbal information. But most dreams are not like that. It is comforting to realize that dreams are rarely literal, so if you have a frightening dream—say, of an accident or death—you should not take it literally.

Since dreams are not literal, how can we conceive of them? We can think of dreams as the result of an energy transaction to deliver information. They are analogous to the way computers translate digital information (strings of 1s and 0s) into typed pages and images. Imagine that the upper levels of the soul leave the body and travel in other dimensions. While there, the soul attracts certain energies that attach to the soul's own energy field.

These energies are processed through what the mystics call the *bat ayin* (literally, "daughter of the eye"), or inner eye. The way the body deals with this energetic information is to form images similar to visual or other sensory images. They filter through the *nefesh*, whose center of energy is in the womb or belly. This is the place of the *sefirot Netzach* and *Hod,* which, the Hasidic masters teach, is the locus of prophecy.[15] The mode of intelligence operating here is expert in metaphor and symbol, which is why dreams are so heavily laden with symbolism and word play.

At some point, either in the dream itself or as we return to a waking state, the brain strings the images together in a form that is familiar and accessible to us, usually a story. When we are fully awake, we can tell or write down the dream.

But the actual message of the dream is the original energy that the soul attracted. We may not be able to bring the energy, or information, completely into consciousness; sometimes we know we were dreaming but can remember nothing about it. Perhaps we have flashes of the dream, but cannot grasp enough of them to put it into words. Sometimes we simply forget the dream immediately after waking. Sometimes it becomes a rich treasury of images. While sometimes a dream is an epiphany, a personal revelation, most of the time it is like archeology. Suddenly we find a shard that seems to have a form and a meaning, even though we do not yet know where it fits.

There's no perfection in dreaming. As the Talmud says, "There is no dream without some nonsense" (*Berachot* 55a). Yet dreams have much sense, too. Remember that a dream's purpose is to help us see more clearly, and that we should pay attention to dreams to help us see dimensions that are not obvious in our waking lives. Remember also that the point of dreaming is not to give us better tools to control the world in an egotistical way. Dreaming is not a technology. Rather, it is a means by which we can allow spiritual reality—ultimately, God—to unfold into the world in a positive way. That is why preparation for sleep is important. The clearer you are when you go into the dream, the more you are a channel for the Divine to unfold in truth and beauty. Do you need to "do" anything about it? Rarely. Probably not. Just trust that remembering your dream will bring us all a step further on the path of conscious evolution.

Dreams Follow Their Interpretation

Abraham, Jacob, Joseph, and many prophets received messages in dreams. Major shifts in Jewish history were presaged by such dreams—the exile of the Jewish people, their preservation in Egypt, their struggles to survive among the nations, the destruction of the Temple and the ultimate renewal of the whole people. Whether on the personal or the collective level, dreams can open us to the future in ways that are often impossible in our busy, constricted waking lives.

But, as the Talmud says, "A dream that is uninterpreted is like a letter unread." If we want to gain more from our dreams, we have to take them seriously. We need to remember them, discuss them, and find ways to approach them so that their spiritual aspects come to the fore. For that purpose, here are some suggestions:

☐ Prepare for dreaming—physically, emotionally, mentally, spiritually—to remind yourself of the sacredness of the dream-world. Physically prepare your bed by smoothing the sheets and arranging the pillows. Treat your body kindly before you sleep with some gentle stretching or massage. Touch the *mezuzah* on the doorpost of your bedroom. Do a forgiveness meditation or prayer to clear your emotional energy. Put pen and paper near your bed to remind yourself to write down the dream. If you customarily read before sleep, choose something spiritual or poetic. Say the prayers of the bedtime *Shema*, at least in abbreviated form.

☐ Keep a dream journal. Writing a dream down validates it as a part of your reality and begins the process of interpretation. If you rarely remember your dreams, or if you only remember fragments of them, still write them down. This tells your mind they are important. Or keep a tape recorder by your bed so you can record your dreams when you wake up.

To remember your dreams better, try to sleep a little longer and/or wake up slowly without moving your body. Staying in the physical position you were in while dreaming can help you capture an image. If you remember even one image, review it a few times in your mind before you move. Give the dream a title. After you have collected several months of dreams, you may want to chart your dreams to discover your personal patterns of dreaming. (See Appendix C for a model of how to do this.)

☐ Tell some of your dreams to a trusted friend or share them in an appropriate environment such as a dream group. As a general rule, we should not try to interpret our own dreams (though you may want to note recurring images).

When you find a friend or group with whom you want to share dreams, remember the important advice of the Talmud and the Zohar: Always give the dream a good turn. Don't judge, challenge, or question the dream. When interpreting another person's dream, try to remove your personal projections from them. Avoid statements like "If this were my dream, I would..." or "When I have this kind of dream, it means ..." Each dreamer's journey is unique. Be open, listening, noncensoring—not only to the dream but to your deeper inner voice that may want to say something to the dreamer. This means listening for the Divine message that is trying to come through. It may be less about the dreamer's daily life or personal relationships than about his or her spiritual destiny. It may be about a larger social or cosmic field than the dreamer usually occupies. The soul is trying to communicate through a language that it hopes you will understand.

Here are a few suggestions about how to begin interpreting dreams:

- ☐ Look at clues that locate the dream. What tells you that this is not ordinary reality? What is the setting and what does it remind you of? Does it feel ancient or contemporary? Personal or collective?

- ☐ What images or words stick in your mind as you listen to the dream? Focus on those more than on trying to interpret the whole "story." If you find one image that rings true, the rest may fall into place.

- ☐ Look for puns and other messages coming through language, as the Talmudic sages did. For example, if an odd or transformed name appears, it may be a pun. Look for hints even in the ordinary names of people and places. For example, if you dream about Providence, Rhode Island, it might be a pun on the idea of Divine Providence rather than a real travel destination.

- ☐ Pay attention to common images, but recognize that you may not immediately know the language your soul is using. If your group starts consistently interpreting a given image in a certain way, the souls of the dreamers may begin to "use" that code. But we can't apply it automatically, like a dictionary definition.

Most of all, bring love, joy, and lightness to your dream interpretations. It's okay to laugh—dreams tickle us because they are so far beyond our waking life.

Let's now consider some frequently asked questions about dreams.

☐ Do recurring dreams mean anything special?

Exact repetitions of dreams are rare, but near-repetitions are fairly common, and repetitions of general themes are not merely common but regular occurrences. When the repetitions are very close to each other and you have been trying to interpret your dreams, it may mean that your soul is telling you that you didn't get the message—try again. Recurrent dreams that are widely spaced in time may be signaling changes in consciousness. Ask yourself when you last had this dream—were you going through changes in your life similar to those you are now facing?

If you suddenly dream about someone you haven't seen in years, it may signal a change in consciousness. This person may be reminding you of certain changes you went through when he or she was an active part of your life. We have discovered that as we go through major changes, we rework parts of our lives, even aspects of ourselves we thought we were done with. Everything significant has to be reintegrated at another level. So if you start dreaming about a difficult relationship that you thought you had settled, it doesn't necessarily mean you need to go back into therapy again. You are rethinking the lessons that you learned, but now from a different perspective.

As for recurrent themes—like going places in a car, bicycle, or airplane—these are often your personal codes for specific kinds of things you are doing in the dream weave. Cars are often our egos or our "karmic" vehicles, symbolizing our physical incarnations. Airplanes could be a pun on "planes," as in different levels. If you have recurrent messengers or guides, you're probably being protected by angels or guided to specific kinds of information.

These clues about themes may—or may not—apply to your dreams. Remember, you have to find your dream's code. Use these as beginning suggestions. When you're on the right track with a dream interpretation, you will know it. Even more, if your soul likes the code you've chosen, it will speak to you in it more and more.

☐ Do we ever dream about past lives?

Some people dream about themselves in past lives with some frequency. When you dream that you are with just one family member in an unusual place, you may be exploring the relationship you had with that person in a past life. When young children have recurring dreams, they may be about past lives. Research has suggested that up until the age of about four, children may remember parts of their previous lives. After that period ends, they may have only fragments that recur as dreams.

☐ What do dreams of destruction and death mean?

If you dream of your own death or near-death, you are probably about to go through a significant transformation. If you dream of someone else's death, it is possible that you should look at the situation your friend is in. If he or she is going through difficulties, it may be a dream of transformation. If there are health issues involved, the dream may be pointing to something that needs attention. Recall that one of the categories the Talmud called "prophetic" is "dreams that a friend has about one." Their purpose is to set in motion forces that could change a situation. Whether there is anything to be acted upon in the waking world depends on the situation.

☐ How do you know if a dream foretells anything?

We usually don't, until later. In fact, prophetic dreams are usually quite densely coded. So even if we suspect that it's prophetic, we rarely know exactly what it is prophesying. If we have dreams of violence and destruction that have no direct referent in our lives, we may be dreaming of forces that are affecting what the mystics call the "upper realms"—forces that will affect life on earth only later, and possibly indirectly.

Dreaming in Community

There is one more very important aspect of dreaming. Dreaming has a collective quality, an aspect that goes beyond the individual. This is difficult to prove or even to describe adequately, but we are convinced that it is so. We meet in dreams to work together on insights that will lead to a better world.

The individual self is not the limit of dreaming, any more than it is the limit of our efforts in waking life. Judaism teaches that we are all ultimately one soul. In waking life, this means that we are all responsible for each other, and we all affect each other whether we realize it or not. In the dream world, this is all the more true. As William Butler Yeats wrote, "In dreams begin responsibility." Without the ego-reinforcing experience of a physical body, the soul is free to be itself, which also means free to be in meaningful relationship with others.

As a result, it should be no surprise that, as we start becoming more conscious of our dreams, we realize that we dream about each other a great deal. We "meet" on the "dream weave" to share and plan. These meetings may or may not be with people you know in your waking life. You may dream of hotels with corridors and elevators and large meeting halls, where it seems that many connections are being made. You may dream of being in a palace, an ancient temple, a retreat center, or a classroom where you seem to be with familiar people even though you do not recognize them.

We've found that when these settings appear in our dreams, we are often dreaming about bigger issues than our own private lives. Sometimes "celebrity" dreams are like that too. You may dream about a world leader or a major spiritual figure because you move in larger circles in the dream world than you do in daily life. When we have dreams that relate to the larger world than our own private sphere, we may or may not come back with specific information to carry into waking life. Let it be enough to know that the collective soul-work is going on, that we are part of a larger community even in our sleep.

A great tapestry is being woven. Each of us has our particular colors, our specific part of the weave. Or, in another metaphor, we are like the stars that appear in the sky beside the moon. Each of us has our particular place, circuit, and ability to give heat and light. But we are also part of constellations from the earthly point of view, and we are part of galaxies that form communities of light in the heavens. As stars, we dream to understand ourselves; but we also dream a larger reality of which we are a part.

When we form dream groups we also create a constellation of energy, and we share a larger vision of reality. With Divine help, we can bring that special way of seeing that we experience in our dreams closer to earth. Ultimately, by paying attention to our dreams, our own "still small voice" will begin to be heard.

Opening Our Inner Eyes

These are a few suggestions that may help you approach sleeping and dreaming with a positive attitude. Dreaming need not arouse fear and anxiety. Approach it with openness and curiosity. When going to bed becomes a sacred ceremony, when dreams become at least as interesting to us as the mundane events of our waking lives, then we may be ready for the Divine message that the prophet Joel received: "I will pour out my spirit on all flesh."

Most importantly, remember that dreaming is designed to nourish us. In Elijah's dream at the beginning of this chapter, he fell asleep and was fed by an angel. The dream-food nourished him for forty days and forty nights. This tells us that Elijah became like Moses, who was able to stay on Mount Sinai for forty days and nights without food when he was receiving the Torah. Elijah, too, was able to go to "the mount of God," where he experienced Divine revelation in the form of the still, small voice.

The dreams of our ancestors and prophets gave birth to and fed a people, a kingdom of *cohanim*, a holy nation. Likewise, dreams can provide us with the sustenance we need to pursue our spiritual paths. We need not be limited by the everyday world, immersed in material concerns or imprisoned by social pressures. Within us, our potential is waiting to come forth. Dreaming can open the channels for that potential to be realized.

In dreaming, we can turn to the light—the light that streams through our souls while the world is dark. Light is the theme of the *Hamapil* prayer. Its blessing is that a loving, protective God will nourish us with an illumination, just as the Divine Light secretly illumines the whole world. The prayer promises us freedom from fear and, with this, the possibility of enlightenment in our dreams. As you say this blessing, know that you are protected and, with Divine love around you, you are ready to surrender to sleep. Imagine that you are opening the gate of the inner eye, so that love, peace, and beauty will be more fully revealed to you.

There are no movements for this prayer, and no words or thoughts to follow it. Eventually, you will learn it by heart so that you can say it after the exterior lights are out, with eyes closed.

Sweet dreams.

בָּרוּךְ אַתָּה יהוה אֱלֹהֵינוּ מֶלֶךְ הָעוֹלָם,

הַמַּפִּיל חֶבְלֵי שֵׁנָה עַל עֵינָי,

וּתְנוּמָה עַל עַפְעַפָּי.

וִיהִי רָצוֹן מִלְּפָנֶיךָ

יהוה אֱלֹהַי וֵאלֹהֵי אֲבוֹתַי,

שֶׁתַּשְׁכִּיבֵנִי לְשָׁלוֹם וְתַעֲמִידֵנִי לְשָׁלוֹם.

וְאַל יְבַהֲלוּנִי רַעְיוֹנַי,

וַחֲלוֹמוֹת רָעִים, וְהִרְהוּרִים רָעִים.

וּתְהֵא מִטָּתִי שְׁלֵמָה לְפָנֶיךָ,

וְהָאֵר עֵינַי פֶּן אִישַׁן הַמָּוֶת.

כִּי אַתָּה הַמֵּאִיר לְאִישׁוֹן בַּת עָיִן.

בָּרוּךְ אַתָּה יהוה,

הַמֵּאִיר לָעוֹלָם כֻּלּוֹ בִּכְבוֹדוֹ.

Baruch Ata, Adonai, Elohenu, Melech haolam,
Hamapil chevlei shena al einai
utenumah al afapai.
Vihi ratzon milfanecha, Adonai Elohai vElohei Avotai,
shetashkivenu leshalom veta'amidenu leshalom.
Ve'al yevahaluni rayonai,
vacholomot ra'im, veharhorim ra'im.
Utehei mitati shelema lifanecha,
veha'er einai pen ishan hamavet.
Ki ata hameir le'ishon bat ayin.
Baruch Ata, Adonai, hameir la'olam kulo bichvodo.

Blessed are You, Adonai our God, Ruler of the Universe,
Who casts the bonds of sleep on my eyes
and slumber on my eyelids.
May it be Your Will, Adonai my God and God of my ancestors,
that You lay us down in peace and raise us up to peace.
May my ideas, bad dreams or evil fantasies not trouble me.
May my bed be complete before You,
and may You illuminate my eyes, lest sleep be death.
For You are the Illuminator of the pupil of the eye.
Blessed are You, Adonai, Who illumines
the whole world with his Glory.

The Bedtime *Shema*: Short Version

We recommend that you study each of the preceding chapters and practice the prayers in full because you will master the intent of each prayer more completely in that way. Yet we also know that sometimes it is difficult to set aside enough time for each prayer. The following capsule summary will help you focus on some crucial elements of the bedtime *Shema* even when you cannot do the whole ceremony.

☐ **Setting Up Your Sacred Space**

Sit on the edge of your bed. Close your eyes and raise your arms to the sides to draw your *sukkah* of peace. Turn your torso gently left and right as you visualize your protective shelter over and around you. Say *Hashkivenu, Adonai Elohenu, leshalom, veha-amidenu, Malkenu, lechayim.* (Lay us down, Lord our God, in peace, and raise us up, our Ruler, to life.)

145

☐ Untie Yourself from Relationships and Problems

Ask God to show you someone whom you need to forgive or from whom you need forgiveness. As the person appears in front of you, see the cord of energy that connects your heart and solar plexus to those of that person. Take three deep breaths. Reach out and untie the cord in the middle. Breathe deeply as your energy returns to your own heart.

☐ Bind Yourself to God

If you wish, you may lie down now. Imagine yourself being comforted by a most loving Presence. Cover your eyes with your right hand and say, *Sh'ma Yisrael, Adonai Elohenu, Adonai Echad.* (Hear, O Israel, *Adonai* is Our God, *Adonai* is One!) In an undertone continue, *Baruch Shem Kevod Malchuto le'olam va'ed.* (Blessed be the Name of the Glory of his Kingdom forever.)

☐ Open Yourself to the Blessing of Your True Nature

Say the first verse of the Priestly Blessing, *Yevarechecha Adonai veyish-marecha.* (May God bless you and guard you.) Visualize yourself being wrapped in a warm cocoon of soft fabric. Say *Ya'er Adonai panav eleicha vichuneka.* (May God make the Divine Face shine on you and be gracious to you.) Imagine a soft light washing you from the top of your head to the soles of your feet. Notice if it has any color. Touch your head, temples, throat, shoulders, heart, hips, and abdomen. Imagine the warm light washing you inside as well. Say *Yisa Adonai panav eleicha veyasem lecha shalom.* (May God lift up the Divine Face toward you and give you peace.)

☐ Step into the Inner Eye of Consciousness

If you have not lain down yet, do so now. Say *Baruch ata, Adonai, Elohenu melech ha'olam, Hamapil chevlei shenah al einai utenumah al afapai.* (Blessed are you, *Adonai* our God, Ruler of the Universe, Who casts the bonds of sleep on my eyes and slumber on my eyelids.) Imagine that you are opening the gate of the inner eye, so that love, peace, and beauty will be more fully revealed to you. Say *Baruch ata, Adonai, hameir la'olam kulo bichevodo*. (Blessed are you, God, who illumines the whole world in Divine Glory.)

These ancient prayers will take you safely into the night. Since the Jewish day begins at night, these are also the first steps you can take toward a good day tomorrow. Just as a restful sleep helps us feel energetic the next morning, so sleep with a spiritual awareness also helps our God-consciousness on the following day. That is what has happened for us over the years. We hope that in sharing this gift with you, the blessings we have received will be greatly increased. May the Bedtime Prayers become one of the important tools on your spiritual path, enriching and deepening your life.

Also, like the moon that shines with its own unique light, the world of dreams offers its special light to us. We hope this book will help make that hidden light more visible for you. When we begin to see the dream world in its true nature, we find that it gives us a way for us all to connect at a different level. It is time to begin telling one another our dreams, so that their hidden light can illuminate all of life. The one-third of life that we spend in sleep can be a treasure, not only of rest from our busy days, but of insight and profound realization. May you find the way to understand the language of your soul in your dreams, so that your own special gifts may shine out clearly to everyone.

Appendix A

The *Shema*

The three paragraphs of the traditional *Shema* are taken from three different passages in Scripture. The first paragraph is known as "accepting the yoke of the Kingdom of Heaven"; the second as "accepting the yoke of the commandments"; the third as the paragraph of the commandment of *tzitzit* (fringes). The last paragraph also fulfills the commandment to remember the exodus from Egypt every day.

Most versions of the bedtime *Shema* use only the first paragraph; some use both the first and the second. The second paragraph is in the plural, addressing the collective "you" (the Jewish people), so it can be considered more appropriate in a public prayer setting. The third focuses on *tzitzit*, which is a *mitzvah* required only in the daytime.

Hear, Israel, Adonai is Our God, Adonai is One! Blessed be the Name of the Glory of his Kingdom forever. You shall love Adonai your God with all your heart, and with all your soul, and with all your resources. These words that I command you today shall be upon your heart. You shall teach them diligently to your children, and speak of them when you are sitting in your house, when you are walking on the road, and when you lie down, and when you rise up. You shall bind them as a sign upon your hand, and they will be as reminders between your eyes, and you shall write them on the doorposts of your house and on your gates.

And it will come to pass, if you diligently obey [literally, deeply hear or fully understand] My commandments that I command you [plural] today, to love Adonai your God and serve God, with all your heart and with all your soul, I will give rain for your land in its time, the early and the late rain, and you will gather in your grain, your wine, and your oil. And I will give grass in the field for your cattle, and you will eat and be satisfied. Watch yourselves lest your heart be lured away and you turn away and serve other gods and bow down to them. For then Adonai's wrath will flare up against you, and God will close the heavens and there will be no rain, and the earth will not yield its produce, and you will swiftly perish from the good land that Adonai gives you. So place these words on you heart and on your vital soul, and bind them for a sign on your hand, and they shall be for reminders between your eyes. You shall teach them to your children, to speak of them when you sit in your house and when you walk on the road, when you lie down and when you rise up. And you shall inscribe them on the doorposts of your house and upon your gates—so that your days and the days of your children will be many on the land that Adonai swore to your fathers to give to them, for as long as the heavens are above the earth.

Adonai spoke to Moses, saying: Speak to the children of Israel and tell them to make for themselves *tzitzit* (fringes) on the corners of their garments throughout their generations, and to attach a thread of blue on the fringe of each corner. They will be *tzitzit* to you and you shall look upon them and remember the commandments of Adonai and fulfill them, and you will not follow after your heart and after your eyes by which you go astray—so that you may remember and fulfill all My commandments and be holy to your God. I am Adonai your God who brought you out of the land of Egypt to be your God; I, Adonai, am your God.

Appendix B

Holy Verses to Soothe Us at Night

If, after saying the Bedtime Prayers, you still cannot fall asleep, you can recite holy verses recommended by the sages. Here are some:

☐ *Torah tziva lanu Moshe morasha kehillat Yaakov.* "Moses commanded us Torah, an inheritance for the congregation of Jacob" (Deuteronomy 33:4), a verse which was traditionally taught to children at an early age.

☐ *Esh tamid tukad al hamizbeach, lo tichbeh.* "A continuous fire shall burn on the altar, it shall not be put out" (Leviticus 6:6). This refers to the flame of devotion in one's heart.

☐ *Or zarua latzaddik, uleyishrei lev simcha.* "Light is sown for the righteous, and joy for the upright in heart" (Psalms 97:11). In Hebrew, the last letter of each word spells out "R. Akiva," referring to the second-century rabbi who was tortured by the Romans and died saying the *Shema* (see Chapter 4). This verse also opens the great *Kol Nidrei* service of Yom Kippur Eve in Orthodox congregations.

☐ *Gad gedud yegudenu, vehu yagud akev. Akev yagud v'hu y'gudenu g'dud Gad.* "Gad will be surrounded by troops, but he will turn them back on their heels. On their heels he will turn them back, the troops that will surround Gad" (Genesis 49:19).

☐ *Im tishkav lo tifchad, veshachabta vearva shenatecha.* "When you lie down, you will not be afraid; you will lie down and your sleep will be sweet" (Proverbs 3:24).

☐ *Lishuatecha kiviti, Adonai.* "For your salvation I hope, Lord" (Genesis 49:18).

☐ *Ata seter li, mitzar titzereni, ronei palet tesoveveni, selah.* "You are a refuge for me; protect me from distress; surround me with songs of deliverance forever" (Psalms 32:7).

☐ *Todieni orach chayim, sova semachot et panecha n'imot biminecha Netzach.* "Make known to me the path of life, satisfy with the joy of Your Face, the bliss of Your right hand forever" (Psalms 16:11).

☐ *Atah takum terachem Tzion, ki et lechenenah, ki va mo'ed.* "Arise and have mercy on Zion, for it is time to be gracious to her, for the appointed time is come" (Psalms 102:14).

☐ *Beyadecha afkid ruchi, paditah oti Adonai El emet.* "Into Your hand I entrust my spirit, You will redeem me, Lord, God of truth" (Psalms 31:6).

Appendix C

Charting the Patterns of Your Dreams

We have learned that it is helpful to discover the patterns of one's own dreaming. You can do this most effectively by charting your dreams according to the phases of the moon and the planets in aspect to the moon (that is, planets occupying positions in the sky that create certain geometric angles to the moon). The details of this method are based on teachings that Connie Kaplan has more fully explained in *A Woman's Book of Dreams* (Portland, Ore.: Beyond Words, 1999). You will need an astrological calendar, available at many bookstores that carry a strong line of spiritual books. This procedure may sound odd, but it's worth noting that Jewish sages have considered astrology potentially valuable in understanding patterns of events happening on earth (however, they advise strongly not to use astrology to predict the future). The Zohar tells us,

> It is incumbent on man to be zealous in searching after wisdom "in the wide places. "This refers to the firmament, which contains all the luminous stars, and which constitutes the fountain of perennial waters .... And there she "utters her voice," both the superior and the lower Wisdom, which in truth are one .... "For ask now of the days past...and from one end of heaven to another" (Deuteronomy 4:32).[1]

What is important here, as Kaplan explains, is that the patterns of the moon are particularly influential on dreams. (If you are a woman who menstruates, you should note on the chart the day your menstrual cycle begins, since your cycle may be influential as well.) Charting your dreams will enable you to discover your own dreaming patterns over long stretches of time. In the meantime, while you are developing the database for your patterns, keeping astrological records reinforces in your mind the idea that dreams are important.

Here is Kaplan's method for charting dreams, which we have successfully used: First give each dream a title. You might do this when you write the dream in your dream journal. Each month, make a circular chart that gives you a picture of your dreaming according to the moon's travels through the zodiac and your personal monthly cycle. After you have collected several months to a year's worth of dreams, you can group dreams according to signs and planetary aspects.

On the facing page is a sample circular chart. You can see that dreams clustered this month in the sign of Taurus, so the dreamer would want to look at Taurus dreams in other months also.

Below the circle is the second kind of chart. Here are listed dreams that occurred when the moon was in aspect to Mercury, over a period of more than a year. Depending on how complicated you want the cross-referencing system to be, you could add the zodiac sign and other planetary aspects, and your own comments, as you begin to see patterns in your dreams. It takes a long period of charting dreams before this method begins to yield clear patterns, but the results can be extremely interesting.

Using both kinds of charting, you will eventually find that certain kinds of dreams occur at certain times of the lunar month, and/or when the moon is influenced by the energies of certain planets. When you have collected groups of dreams that are related to each other in this way, you will be able to interpret them with greater depth of understanding.

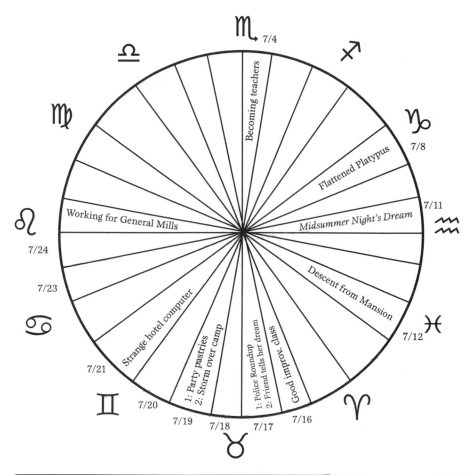

MERCURY	DATE	NOTES
Weaving (Hilton ceiling)	6-20-7	
Campfire Girls	7-14-7	
R. & Tower David	9-1-7	Children
Yosemite/bird in tallit	9-6-7	Animals
Lie down with Sally	11-15-7	*Sally—see 5/24 Merc*
Avraham & Sara grave R'O.	12-8-7	
Weft foundation	12-7-7P*	
Paradise/sterility	1-3-8 S	
Teaching closed down	6-15-8	School
Learn in "good" improv class	7-16-8	School
Police Roundup	7-18-8	*See police dream 10-9*
Bangdangling dance	8-4-8	

Notes

Quotations from the Zohar in this book are based on the classic five-volume English translation by Sperling and Simon (Soncino Press, 1946). In these endnotes, they will be cited with the volume number of the Sperling and Simon translation, followed by the folio number cited by the translators and the page number of the English edition.

All quotations from the Talmud are from the Babylonian Talmud unless otherwise noted.

Chapter 1

1. The fraction "one-sixtieth" is a standard Talmudic formula indicating an amount that is significant even though it seems very tiny. For example, the quantity of milk that can make a pot of soup into a dairy soup is one-sixtieth. Conversely, a small part of something can be described as "one-sixtieth," meaning that its essence is the same as the larger entity, even though other things may be mixed in. "Shabbat is one-sixtieth of the World to Come" is a good example: Shabbat partakes of the

essence of the World to Come, but in the present world there are still many obstacles (*kelipot*) mingled with that pure essence.

2. Judaism includes a belief in a negative experience after death, called *Gehinnom* or *Gehenna*. This was a temporary way station, a place of purification, on the way to *Gan Eden*. On Jewish beliefs about death and the afterlife, see Neil Gillman, *The Death of Death: Resurrection and Immortality in Jewish Thought* (Woodstock, Vt.: Jewish Lights, 1997), and Simcha Paul Raphael, *Jewish Views of the Afterlife* (Northvale, N.J.: Jason Aronson, 1994).

3. This line of thought derives from sections of the Zohar and was conveyed through Rabbi Isaac Luria, the leading teacher in sixteenth-century Sfat in northern Israel, and Rabbi Moshe Chaim Luzzatto of seventeenth-century Italy, to most branches of modern Hasidism. Here is a quotation from Luzzatto's *The Way of God* (*Derech Hashem*) part 3, section 1, paragraph 4:

> Even though this Divine Soul is often referred to as a single entity, it actually consists of a number of parts on different levels. We can therefore say that there are actually a number of souls, bound together like links in a chain .... Each of these levels is bound to the one below it, until the lowest one is bound to the animal soul, which in turn is linked to the blood.
>
> It is possible for some of these parts of the soul to remove themselves at various times and later return. It is also possible that levels add themselves to a person's soul and then leave. All this can happen with absolutely no visible effect on the body .... The soul is thus divided into five parts. They are the *Nefesh* (Soul), *Ruach* (Spirit), *Neshamah* (Breath), *Chayah* (Living Essence) and *Yechidah* (Unique Essence).

The terminology in this book differs somewhat from the above translation. We refer to *neshamah* as "soul" and *nefesh* as "vital force."

4. Luzzatto, *Way of God*, 187. The radical theoretical biologist Rupert Sheldrake suggested that living things interact with what he calls "morphic fields," a kind of energy field around each organism that pulls it, so to speak, toward growth and higher levels of complexity. Study of this concept may offer an appropriate parallel for understanding at least the lower levels of the soul.

5. Ibid, 189. Luzzatto says that the portions from *ruach* and upwards all rise and sever themselves from the body, leaving only the *nefesh* in contact with the animal soul. Here is how the Zohar describes this process (Zohar I:83a–83b, 277–78):

> The words "With my soul have I desired You in the night" refer to the *nefesh* that has sway by night, while the words "with my spirit within me will I seek You early" refer to the *ruach* that has sway by day. *Nefesh* and *ruach* are not two separate grades, but one grade with two aspects. There is still a third aspect that should dominate these two and cleave to them as they to it, which

is called "higher spirit" (*neshamah*) .... *Nefesh* is the lowest stirring, it supports and feeds the body and is closely connected with it. When it sufficiently qualifies itself, it becomes the throne on which rests the lower spirit, or *ruach*, as it is written, "until the spirit be poured on us from on high" (Isaiah 32:15). When both have prepared themselves sufficiently, they are qualified to receive the higher spirit, *neshamah*, to which the lower spirit, *ruach*, becomes a throne and which is undiscoverable, supreme over all.

Nefesh is also compared to the dark light at the bottom of a candle flame (the blue flame), *ruach* is like the white light above it, and both are a throne for "a light that cannot be fully discerned, an unknown something resting on that white light."

Rabbi Nachman of Breslov explains that the soul itself is renewed during sleep. Clearly, the essence of the soul is divine and does not go through periods of tiredness. He is referring to the level of the *neshamah*, which is connected to human intellect. He says that when a person is tired—or in another form of constricted consciousness such as confusion—the *mochin* (mentalities) or intellectual aspects of the soul, need to be renewed. This happens through sleep, when the soul ascends to the *sefirah Malkhut*. *Malkhut* clears the soul of negative forces (*kelipot*) so that it can receive the protective garment of *Binah*, which renews the glow of the heart and its understanding (the *chashmal* of Ezekiel's vision) through the Light of the Divine Face. For further discussion, see Rabbi Nachman of Breslov, *Likutey Moharan Vol. 5 (Lessons 33–48)*, translated by Moshe Mykoff, annotated by Chaim Kramer, edited by Moshe Mykoff and Ozer Bergman (Jerusalem and New York: Breslov Research Institute, 1997), #35, 105–108, text and notes.

Rabbi Nachman's brief summary of the nighttime mystical ascent in this lesson remarkably summarizes the whole bedtime *Shema*. The clearing of negative forces comes through the forgiveness prayer; the saying of the *Shema* connects us through faith to *Malkhut*, Jerusalem, and the moon; the Priestly Blessing invokes the Divine Face; and the *Hamapil* prayer turns the soul to its Source of illumination.

6. As Luzzatto puts it (*Way of God*, 189), "When these higher levels of the soul perceive something, they can sometimes transmit it, step by step, until it reaches the animal soul. The imagination is then stimulated and forms images in the normal manner. [A person can then see this as a dream.]"

7. R. T. Pivik, "The Several Qualities of Sleepiness: Psychophysiological Considerations," in *Sleep, Sleepiness and Performance*, edited by Timothy H. Monk (New York: John Wiley & Sons), 17. He goes on to assert that "the cognitive changes occurring at this time may actively facilitate the sleep onset process" (p. 21); in other words, it is necessary to let the normal rational processes shut down. The state of sleep research is indicated by Pivik's summary that "the details of the complex processes involved in the transitions between sleep and wakefulness continue to elude us. Still, it is clear that the central nervous system undergoes a major reorganization as it shifts back and forth between wakefulness and sleep, and it is also obvious that this reorganization is structured to normally take place over an

extended period of time" (p. 28). Bedtime rituals aid this process by allowing gradual rather than sudden shifts in the nervous system, so that heart and respiration are not adversely affected.

8. Insomnia was known in ancient times, so it is not merely a product of modern culture. Today, one-third of Americans are afflicted with some form of insomnia, including difficulty falling asleep, waking up and being unable to return to sleep, and early waking. In addition, many people use sleep-inducing substances such as alcohol, extra food, or medication, or they drive themselves to exhaustion in order to fall asleep. Researchers know that these disorders appear most often in connection with anxiety or depression, but there are no clear lines of causation. Sleep research tells us that if you're having problems in your daytime life, you may have problems at night, too. This is hardly a surprising conclusion!

    The shift into sleep is a very important shift in consciousness. This shift appears to be part of the inherent programming of the human brain. It's not merely a natural result of physical tiredness, as sleep research has shown. What is known is that if we do not get enough sleep, cerebral functions begin to suffer. For a discussion of types of sleep, see James A. Horne, "Dimensions to Sleepiness," in Monk , *op. cit.* 169–180. According to Horne, the cerebrum may well have some essential requirement for sleep, especially what he calls core sleep, made up of four or five hours that includes certain amounts of deep sleep (known as Stage 4) and REM (or rapid eye movement) sleep. This enables the cerebrum to go "off-line" and detach from sensory input.

    The purpose of sleep for the health of the intellectual faculties was well-known to Jewish teachers and healers, and getting as much sleep as we need for clear mental functioning is considered a *mitzvah*. For example, Rabbi Nachman of Breslov taught that sleep was essential to restore the powers of the intellect. See *Likutey Moharan 35* and commentary.

9. Zohar I:12b, 51–52.

10. Zohar I:34a, 128.

11. Why the (half-) *Hallel* should be recited on Rosh Chodesh, which is not a full holiday with abstinence from work, was a question for the sages. It seems to be based primarily on a custom that arose in the Diaspora. One explanation is that the twelve exclamations of *Hallelu* (Praise Him) in the last Psalm of King David (Psalm 150) refer to the twelve new moons of the year, while the customary repetition of the last verse reminds us of the additional new moon in a leap year. Another is that the *Hallel* sings of the reestablishment of the Davidic lineage, because its revival is symbolically linked with the renewal of the moon. Still another is that there were so many incidents of danger followed by deliverance that it became a custom to thank God for the deliverances every month. See the discussion in Elie Munk, *The World of Prayer, Vol. II: Sabbath and Festival Prayers* (New York: Feldheim, 1987), 86.

12. God's love for the Jewish people is alluded to in the comparison with the moon.

Thus the Zohar (II:199a, 255):

> After God created the moon he had her constantly before his eyes (Deuteronomy 11:12). In regard to this it is also written, "He saw it and declared it (*vayesaprah*), he established it, yes, and searched it out" (Job 28:27). He saw it means that through his providence the sun is reflected in it. The term *vayesaprah* we may translate, "He made it like sapphire." "He established it" so that it should fall properly into twelve divisions [twelve months compared to twelve tribes] ... and searched it out—to guard it.

13. Munk, *World of Prayer Vol. II*, 92. Munk has a unique understanding of the Rosh Chodesh offering as Israel's response to the guilt it feels at not having yet changed its status among the nations.

14. Zohar II:136a, 48.

15. On a microcosmic level, the mystics held that an individual can "restore" the moon and reunite it with the sun through marriage and appropriate sexuality. This is alluded to many times in the Zohar. One example (Zohar II:196b, 246): "'That is thy portion in life [with your wife]' (Ecclesiastes 9:9) alludes to the association of the sun with the moon, as it behooves us to bring the moon into the sun and the sun into the moon as it were, so that there should be no separation between them, this being the portion of man by which he may enter the World to Come."

16. A full version is in Talmud *Chullin* 60b. Different versions, even more negative toward the moon, appear in the Zohar. Another is quoted, in excerpts by Rabbi Eliyahu Dessler, in *Strive for Truth* (English translation of *Michtav Me-Eliyahu* by Aryeh Carmell; New York: Feldheim, 1989), part 2, 91. He interprets the midrash as referring to the strife inevitable in this world. This became a major theme in such classic medieval texts as the Zohar. There, the smallness of the moon is not merely about the ups and downs of history, but is also connected to the victory of the "evil serpent" over *Chava* in the Garden of Eden, and to the diminution of women. All these are in turn associated with the "left side" in Kabbalah, or, as we would call it in modern psychology, the "dark side," full of the dangerous unknown.

    The sun or masculine side of God is affected as well. The Zohar says that when the Temple was destroyed and the *Shekhinah* went into exile, the masculine side of God "withdrew his light and became altered from what he was, as it is written: 'The sun was darkened in his going forth' (Isaiah 13:10) ... and '... I clothe the heavens with blackness, and I make sackcloth their covering' (Isaiah 50:3) .... All the souls that issued then were not the same as they had been when the sun was in union with the moon" (Zohar II:182a–182b, 196–97).

17. Zohar II:168b, 156.

18. Zohar II:142a, 145. This is a different line of interpretation from that which usually associates Isaac with *mincha*, the afternoon prayer, as the time of judgment. See Elie Munk, *World of Prayer*, 9.

19. Zohar I:92b, 304.

20. Ibid. Joseph gave the largest portion (thirty-seven years) because he was "reckoned the equivalent of the other two ... and he was better able than the others to illumine the moon."

21. See notes to Rabbi Nachman of Breslov's *Likutey Moharan 35*.

22. Yitzhak Buxbaum, *Jewish Spiritual Practices* (Northvale, N.J.: Jason Aronson, 1990), 534–38. His quotations are from Adin Steinsaltz, *The Long Shorter Way*, 240, and Tzadok Hacohen of Lublin, *Tzidkat Hatzaddik #238*. See also Rabbi Nachman of Breslov, *Likutey Moharan Vol. 5, #35*, 103n.

> The *Maharal* (Rabbi Loew of Prague) stated his firm opinion that we should not stay up at night to do secular work. See his commentary to *Pirkei Avot* (*Sayings of the Fathers*).

23. Zohar I:82b, 274–75. Cf. the following (Zohar I:92b, 304):

> Midnight I will rise to give thanks to You because of Your righteous judgments (Psalms 119:62). Since the word "at" is omitted, we may take "Midnight" as an appellation of The Holy-One-Blessed-Be-He, who is addressed thus by David because He is to be found with His retinue at midnight, that being the hour when He enters the Garden of Eden to converse with the righteous.
>
> Said Rabbi Abba to Rabbi Jacob, "Truly we have now an opportunity to associate with the *Shekhinah*." So they went and sat by him, and said to him, "Repeat what you just said, for it is excellent. Where did you get it from?"
>
> He replied, "I learned it from my grandfather." He told me that during the first three hours of the night the accusing angels below are actively going about the world, but at midnight precisely God enters the Garden of Eden and the accusations below cease. These nightly ceremonies above take place only at midnight precisely (cf. Genesis 14:15, Exodus 12:29) .... David knew this, because—so the old man told me—his kingship depended on this; and therefore he used to rise at this hour and chant praises, and for this reason he addressed God as "Midnight." He also said, "I rise to give thanks to You for Your righteous judgments," because this is the fount of justice, and the judgments of earthly kings derive from here; therefore David never neglected to rise and sing praises at this hour.

24. Rabbi Yitzhak Isaac of Kamorna, *Ateret Tiferet*, p. 37, #49, quoted in Buxbaum, *Jewish Spiritual Practices*, 535.

25. Buxbaum, *Jewish Spiritual Practices*, 563.

26. Zohar II:217b, 306.

27. Zohar I:83a, 277. The Talmud speaks of the "watches" of the night as being parallel to those of the day. Talmud *Berachot* 3a: "There are watches in heaven as well

as on earth. Rabbi Eliezer says, 'The night has three watches, and at each watch the Holy-One-Blessed-Be-He sits and roars like a lion ....' [On earth,] in the first watch the ass brays; in the second, the dogs bark; in the third, the child sucks from the breast of his mother, and the woman talks with her husband." The mystics later expand on this to describe different spiritual potentials that exist at different times of night. The beginning of the night is the time when *shaidim* (demons) are up and about; midnight is when the righteous join God in *Gan Eden*; after midnight, the various *sefirot* move about—presumably bringing information down through the worlds.

28. Timothy H. Monk explains the importance of ritual in his article, "Circadian Aspects of Subjective Sleepiness: A Behavioural Messenger?" in Monk, *Sleep, Sleepiness and Performance,* 39–64.

> Unlike the playful young puppy who simply drops in its tracks whenever and wherever sleep overtakes it, healthy human beings often have an elaborate bedtime ritual, setting the stage both mentally and physically for a restful night of sleep. Indeed, some forms of insomnia can be usefully treated by actively developing and practicing such rituals—a concept known as Sleep Hygiene. Because of our free will and active mental life, the human circadian system needs some messenger to tell the conscious mind to begin that bedtime ritual, and to deliver to the mind ever increasing negative sanctions should its "wishes" be ignored. At a certain level these changes induce an "I'm tired and I want to go to bed" feeling—a feeling that is reinforced by ever increasing decrements in performance at all but the most interesting of tasks. Thus, the bedtime ritual is started and the bedtime patterning required by the circadian system becomes the one actively desired by the individual (p. 46).

Monk follows accepted views in stating that the human body's "day" is closer to twenty-five hours than to the earth's solar day of twenty-four hours, and theorizes that because of this, the body needs to be coached so its rhythms remain consistent with the patterns of night and day. Some people need strong cues, others milder ones, to reset their biological clocks to coincide with solar rhythms (pp. 46–47). However, the "25-hour day" theory has recently been called into question, so this might not be an appropriate explanation of the need for bedtime rituals as cues.

Interestingly, the Jewish evening prayers in the synagogue include a blessing that specifically tells us to pay attention to the solar day. We address thanks to God who "rolls away darkness from before light, and light from before darkness," as a cue to begin closing down our personal day. See also Pivik, "Several Qualities," 21.

Cynthia M. Dorsey elucidates other mechanisms used in treating sleep disorders in her article "Failing to Sleep: Psychological and Behavioral Underpinnings of Insomnia," in Monk, *Sleep, Sleepiness and Performance,* 223–247. Cognitive treatments include diminishing pre-sleep worry (about the day's events or tomorrow's plans) by replacing it with thoughts more compatible with relaxation and sleep. Self-suggestion and imagery are used, especially images of warmth and heaviness.

Meditation is also helpful, especially when it focuses on the rhythm of respiration and repetition of a "mantra." This is interesting in light of some Bedtime Prayers traditions of repeating certain verses three times each. One of these has a frequent repetition of the consonant sounds "g" and "d," which suggest heaviness (see Appendix B).

Other methods use progressive relaxation or biofeedback to produce physiological calm. However, Dorsey notes that researchers have been unable to demonstrate a definite relationship between improving sleep and physical calm. The beneficial effects of muscle relaxation and biofeedback operate in some other way than physiological. In our view, these results appear because it is not the muscles that need sleep, but the cerebrum. Shifts in mental consciousness caused by relaxation training or biofeedback are more crucial than any measurable effect on the physiology of the body.

29. One opinion holds that scholars whose main occupation is studying Torah need not do this, but even they should say a verse from Psalms: "Into Your hand I commit my spirit. You have redeemed me, O Lord, You God of truth" (Psalms 31:6).

30. Buxbaum, *Jewish Spiritual Practices,* 547–58.

31. However, if we cannot fall asleep, repeating holy verses is recommended. See Appendix B.

Chapter 2

1. Rabbi Nosson Scherman, note to translation in the *Artscroll Siddur* (Brooklyn, N.Y.: Mesorah Publications, 1980), 263.

2. Rabbi Abraham Isaac Kook, *Olat Reiyah*, Vol. I (Jerusalem: Mossad HaRav Kook, 1983), 418. This is Rav Kook's Commentary to the *Siddur*.

3. Ibid.

4. Zohar II:168a, 163a, 144, 124.

5. Munk, *World of Prayer,* 205.

6. *Artscroll Siddur (Ashkenaz),* 295.

7. Ibid., 423.

8. Adin Steinsaltz, *The Thirteen Petaled Rose*, translated by Yehuda Hanegbi (New York: Basic Books, 1980), 8–9:
   An angel is a spiritual reality with its own unique content, qualities, and

character.... The substantial quality of an angel may be an impulse or a drive—say, an inclination in the direction of love or a seizure of fear, or pity, or the like. To express a larger totality of being, we may refer to a "camp of angels." In the general camp of love, for example, there are many subdivisions, virtually innumerable shades and gradations of tender feeling.... Whereas among human beings emotions change and vary either as persons change or according to the circumstances of time and place, an angel is totally the manifestation of a single emotional essence.

9. Ibid., 11:

    The person who performs a *mitzvah*, who prays or directs his mind toward the Divine, in so doing creates an angel, which is a sort of reaching out on the part of man to the higher worlds. Such an angel...connected in its essence to the man who created it, still lives... in a different dimension of being, namely in the world of formation.... This is the process by which the specific message or offering to God that is intrinsic in the *mitzvah* rises upward and introduces changes in the system of the higher worlds—foremost in the world of formation. From here, in turn, they influence the worlds above them.

10. Ibid., 26–29.

11. Buxbaum, *Jewish Spiritual Practices*, 549–50.

Chapter 3

1. Usually the Prayer of Forgiveness is at the very beginning of the Bedtime Prayers. We place it after the *Hashkivenu* because we have found it best to use the words and movements of this prayer, which create an angelic *sukkah* of peace and safety, to frame the entire sacred space of the Bedtime Prayers. In addition, this placement makes sense because the *Hashkivenu* is imported from the synagogue prayers that are said earlier in the evening.

2. The traditional prayer says "every Jew" (*kol yehudi*) rather than everyone, but the remainder of the sentence is couched in universal terms: "no person (*adam*) be punished."

3. Simon Weisenthal, *The Sunflower* (New York: Schocken Books, 1994). For a variety of discussions of the issue of forgiveness, see Lewis B. Smedes, *The Art of Forgiving* (New York: Ballantine Books, 1995); Earnie Larsen, *From Anger to Forgiveness* (New York: Ballantine Books, 1992); and Beverly Flanigan, *Forgiving the Unforgivable* (New York: IDG Books, 1994) and *Forgiving Yourself* (New York: IDG Books, 1997).

4. For many sources discussing the importance of reviewing one's day and forgiving others before sleep, see Buxbaum, *Jewish Spiritual Practices,* 539–547.

5. For an excellent discussion and a model for understanding, see Simcha Paull Raphael, *Jewish Views of the Afterlife,* 376–77. Examples from the Zohar are discussed on pp. 290–91, and also appear in a Hasidic story, pp. 394–97. For a discussion of *Gehenna* (or *Gehinnom*), *Gan Eden,* and the soul's return to its Source, see pp. 298–314 and 384–394.

6. For a thorough discussion, see Rabbi Eliyahu E. Dessler, "Discourse on Free Will," *Strive for Truth!* (*Michtav me-Eliyahu*), Vol. 2, translated by Aryeh Carmell (New York: Feldheim, 1985).

7. Rabbi Abraham Isaac Kook, *Celebrations of the Soul: The Holidays in the Life and Thought of Rabbi Abraham Isaac Kook,* translated and adapted by Pesach Jaffe (Jerusalem: Genesis Jerusalem Press, 1992), 61.

Chapter 4

1. These are #2 and #3 among the positive commandments in his *Sefer Hamitzvot,* which lists the commandments in their logical order of priority. (The first is believing in God as the Creator and Sustainer of the universe.)

2. *The Bedtime Shema* (Brooklyn, N.Y.: Mesorah Publications, 1995), *xiv*.

3. Rabbi Yitzchak Ginsburgh, *The Alef-Beit: Jewish Thought Revealed Through the Hebrew Letters* (Northvale, N.J.: Jason Aronson, 1995), sections on *mem, ayin,* and *shin*.

4. Rabbi Nachman of Breslov brings a fascinating teaching on this point based on the *gematria*. The numerical value of the letters of the *Shema* total 410. This is the same as the value of the letters in *ChaShMaL LeV,* the glow of the heart. *Chashmal* is a term found in Ezekiel's famous vision of the Chariot. This word describes the glowing center of the brightness that he saw in his vision, coming from the area of the heart. Rabbi Nachman teaches, based on Zohar 2:203b, that when we speak truth from the heart, and when we say the *Shema* with *kavannah* (spiritual intent), we awaken a force in our hearts—the *chashmal*—that subdues the evil forces, or *kelipot*. This is all the more true of the bedtime saying of the *Shema,* which follows the forgiveness prayer when we have cleared our hearts. See Rabbi Nachman of Breslov, *Likutey Moharan 5,* #35, 115n.

5. Rabbi Adolf Altmann, Chief Rabbi of Trier, "The Meaning or Soul of 'Hear, O Israel,'" translated by Barbara R. Algin, in *Jewish Values in Jungian Psychology,* edited by Levi Meier (Lantham: University Press of America, 1991), 61; quoted in Lamm, *Shema,* 14–15.

6. Ultimately this codification was completed by Rabbi Yehudah Hanasi (Judah the

Prince) around the year 200, in the form we now know as the Mishnah. However, earlier sages including Akiva had begun their own compilations, which may have been used as sources for the final Mishnah.

7. The Talmud tells the story of Akiva's death in *Berachot* 61b.

8. On this aspect of Rabbi Akiva's death, see Rabbi Avraham Yitzchak Kook, *Olat Reiyah*, 250.

9. The commentators note that in his statement, "what will befall you" would normally be written *yikrah lahem*, but here it is written *yikra lahem*, with the letter alef instead of the letter heh. So it actually means, "what will call to you in the latter days." In other words, he reveals what your calling will be. See *The Stone Chumash* (Brooklyn, N.Y.: Mesorah Publications, 1995), note to Genesis 49:1, 275.

10. Zohar I:90b–91a, 298.

11. In the daily prayer services, this is followed by two more passages taken from different sections of the Torah. We are limiting our discussion to the first paragraph only. See Appendix A for the full text of the *Shema*.

12. Rabbi Nachman of Breslov, *Likutey Moharan 5*, #35, 105–108, text and notes. Mystically, he explains, the bedtime *Shema* clears the way for the soul to ascend, and it is supervised on its journey by the *sefirah Malkhut*, which is associated with King David, the moon, and the *Shekhinah*. He also associates it with Jerusalem, the "small city," which is like the moon, the "small light." In other words, the soul does not jump directly to its root in the *sefirah Chochmah* or *Keter* but is guided, as it were, by *Malkhut*, to *Bina*, the Divine Mother, and then reconnected to *Chochmah*. This is the process of renewal of the soul during sleep.

13. For the paragraphs that follow the authors are deeply indebted to the insightful discussion in Rabbi Norman Lamm, *Shema: Law and Spirituality in Judaism* (New York: Jewish Publication Society, 1998).

14. Lamm, *Shema*, 29.

15. Rabbenu Yonah, *Sefer Hayirah*, quoted in Lamm, *Shema*, 40.

16. The radical view that nothing exists except God—held by Rabbi Schneur Zalman of Liadi (author of the Tanya, founder of Chabad) and Rabbi Chaim of Volozhin (spokesman for *Mitnagdim*)—is discussed at length in Lamm, *Shema*, under "Kabbalistic Interpretations."

17. Lamm, *Shema*, 54, quoting Rabbi Tzvi Hirsch of Ziditchov.

18. Here is the full quotation from the Zohar (I:12a, 50–51):

    [The third basic precept is] to acknowledge that there is a God, all-powerful and ruler of the universe, and to make due proclamation of his unity every day, as extending in the six supernal directions, and to unify them all through the six words contained in the *Shema Yisrael*, and in reciting these to devote oneself wholly to God.

The word *Echad* therefore must be dwelt on to the length of six words. This is implied in the passage, "Let the waters under the heaven be gathered together unto one place": that is, let the levels beneath the heaven be unified in it so as to form one whole, perfect in all the six directions.

With God's unity one must further associate awe, for which reason one must dwell on the *dalet*, the last letter of *Echad*, the *dalet* being for that reason written larger than the other letters. And this is implied in the words "and let the dry land be seen"; that is, let the *dalet*, which is a "dry land," be associated with that unity.

After forming this union on high it is necessary to repeat the process for the lower world through all its multiplicity in the six lower directions. This is expressed in the verse we recite after the *Shema*, namely, *Baruch shem kevod malchuto l'olam va'ed*, which contains another six words expressive of the unity. In this way, what was dry land becomes fertile soil to produce fruits and flowers and trees. This is implied in the passage, "And God called the dry land earth," that is, by the manifestation of God's unity here below, the earth was duly perfected.

It is for this reason that in the account of the third day the expression "that it was good" appears twice, once for the manifestation of the unity above and once for the manifestation of the unity below. As soon as that unity was made manifest at both ends, the text says, "Let the earth put forth grass," that is, the earth was then fitted to produce fruits and flowers according to its capacity.

19. Rabbi Abraham Isaac Kook, *Olat Reiyah,* Vol. I, 249.

20. Summarized in Artscroll commentary, *Stone Chumash*, note 5 to Deuteronomy 6:5.

21. *Tanya: Likutei Amarim I (Sefer Shel Benonim)*, 229.

22. Rabbi Eleazar in Zohar I:12a, 50.

23. Ibid., 233.

24. Rav Kook points out (*Olat Reiyah*, 249) that the three aspects of ourselves mentioned in the *Shema*—*bechol levavecha uvechol nafshecha uvechol me'odecha*—can be understood in this more inward way. Usually, we read "heart" and "soul" as being inward, while *me'odecha* is usually read as referring to physical strength or resources. He suggests, on the contrary, that *me'odecha* actually refers to the *neshamah*, or highest level of the three, which cannot be contained in the physical vessel of the body, but only felt as sparks of intelligence. These sparks are the "more" of *me'odecha* (*me'od* usually means "very," as in *tov me'od*, "very good").

Chapter 5

1. Rabbis Avie Gold and Nosson Scherman, *Bircas Cohanim: The Priestly Blessings* (Brooklyn, N.Y.: Mesorah Publications, 1981), 27.

2. Gold and Scherman, *Bircat Cohanim,* 27.

3. *Midrash Rabba Numbers, Vol. I,* translated by Judah Slotkin (London: Socino Press, 1939): 11:5, 432–40, offers a discussion of the blessing and suggests passages from *Tanach* (Bible) where one may find examples of each blessing. It compares the first section to Deuteronomy 7:14, implying a blessing of wealth, children, and personal safety and health, and adds also that this blessing guards one from the *yetzer hara* (one's own evil inclination; cf. Proverbs 3:236, Psalms 121:4ff.) and from demons (cf. Psalms 91:7, 11). "Guarding" also suggests that one is guarded until the End, protecting the soul in the hour of death (1 Samuel 25:29, 2:9).

   "May the Lord cause the Divine Face to illuminate you and be gracious to you" is interpreted variously as a blessing for the Torah, for knowledge and understanding, for raising up prophets in the midst of the people, for liberation, for the granting of personal desires, and for the light of the *Shekhinah* (Isaiah 60:1, Psalms 36:10, Psalms 118:27, Isaiah 30:19, Zechariah 12:10, Isaiah 33:2).

   "May the Lord lift up the Divine countenance upon you ..." has the greatest variety of interpretation. It may mean that God's indignation be removed, that God accept us, or that we be made fruitful (Leviticus 20:6, Genesis 19–21, Deuteronomy 10:17, Leviticus 26:9). According to the midrash, Rabbi Nathan says that this is a blessing for the peace of David's house (Isaiah 9:6), while Rabbi says it is the peace of Torah (Psalms 29:11). Rabbi Shimeon ben Halafta is the source that states that it seals the blessing, while Rabbi Eleazar HaKappar says that it seals the whole *tefillah* (prayer), probably referring to the *Amidah,* and that even if there is idol-worship among the Jewish people but they are at peace with one another, evil will not touch them. The midrash also cites Isaiah 57:19 to indicate that angels greet the righteous with a blessing of peace, "'Let him enter into peace' (Isaiah 57: 2). This means to let them rest in their beds, each one in uprightness."

4. *Pirkei Avot (Sayings of the Fathers)* 1:12.

5. The focus on "sealing" at the close of the day is similar to what happens in the daily prayers. In the *Amidah,* the Priestly Blessing occurs at the end of the *modim* (thanksgiving) prayer, the next-to-last section of the *Amidah,* which is not a request but a prayer of gratitude. It links this prayer to the last section, *Sim shalom,* which is a prayer for peace. The Priestly Blessing itself encapsulates the prayer for peace.

6. The blessing is performed with the priests lifting their hands (under their prayer shawls) as if placing them on the heads of the congregation. Elie Munk explains that because the written text (singular) diverges from the masoretic reading (plural), the right hand should be slightly higher than the left, and the two thumbs should touch one another. (In the rare instances when the written Torah text

diverges from the oral reading passed down by tradition, these differences have their own further interpretations—in this case a ritual one.) According to opinions based on midrashic traditions, the middle and ring fingers of each hand should be touching one another, so that there will be only five spaces (two on each side and one formed by the two thumbs and forefingers). According to another opinion, that of the Vilna Gaon and the Zohar, the ten fingers are kept apart from one another, symbolizing the ten *sefirot*. See Munk, *World of Prayer,* Vol. II, 127–128.

7. Ibid., 128.

8. Rabbi Bibi in the name of Rabbi Eleazar, *Midrash Rabba:* Numbers I, 11:3, 421–425.

9. Rabbi Abraham Isaac Kook, *Olat Reiyah*, Vol. I, 419–420.

10. *Midrash Rabba:* Numbers I, 11:3, 421–425, citing Rabbi Meir and Rabbi Jose. Rabbi Samlai, said that the number 60 refers to 24 priestly watches plus 24 Levitical watches plus the twelve tribes of Israel. See Chronicles 24:4, 25:1ff, 27:1 for references to the watches. Rabbi Zeira and Rabbi Judah said in the name of Rabbi Shmuel that the impeccability referred to was that of the scholars who taught the priests, so that the sacrifices would not be unfit.

11. The term "surrounding," sometimes translated as "encompassing" or "encircling," is somewhat misleading. It sounds as if it referred to something external, but the opposite is the case. Rabbi Schneur Zalman of Liadi explains this as follows (*Likutei Amarim: Tanya* [Brooklyn, N.Y.: Kehot Publication Society, 1981], Chapter 48, 251–253):

    > The hidden and concealed light … is of an infinite order and does not clothe itself or exercise its influence in the worlds, to animate them in a revealed manner, but it "encompasses" them from above and is called *sovev kol almin* (the Encompasser of All Worlds). The meaning of this is not that it encircles or encompasses them from above spatially, God forbid, for in spiritual matters the category of space is in no way applicable…. Because the worlds belong in the order of the finite and limited, it follows that only an extremely minute and contracted reflection of the flow of the light of the blessed *En Sof* clothes and reveals itself in them in a revealed form [this is *male kol almin*, Filler of All Worlds] …. But the principal light without contraction to such an extent is called *makif* (encircler) and *sovev* (encompasser) …. Any influence of a concealed nature is referred to as "Encircling from above," for the "hidden world" is on a higher plane than the "revealed world" (emphasis added).

    In other words, the term "encompassing" or "surrounding" is used to indicate that this "light" is a higher level of reality, less contracted and limited, and not to indicate that it is physically exterior.

12. Rabbi Stephen Robbins, "Birkat Cohanim: A Unified Field of Being," in *Learn Torah With … 1995–1996*, edited by Rabbi Stuart Kelman and Joel Grishaver (Los Angeles: Alef Design Group, 1999), 296–272.

13. *Likutei Amarim: Tanya*, Chapter 22, 91.

14. Zohar II:142b, 57.

15. Zohar I:87a, 290–291: " 'Blessed is Abram' corresponds to 'blessed art Thou.' 'To the most High God' to 'O Lord our God.' 'Possessor of heaven and earth' corresponds to 'King of the Universe.' "

16. See Cornelius Van Dam, *The Urim and Thummim: A Means of Revelation in Ancient Israel* (Winona Lake, Ind.: Eisenbrauns, 1997), Chapter 11 and pages 271–273.

    In *Meditation and the Bible* (New York: Samuel Weiser, 1978), Rabbi Aryeh Kaplan observes that this is confirmed by examination of the etymological relationships of the word *choshen*, or breastplate. The root *chash* is the basis of terms such as *nachash* and *lachash*, which pertain to different types of divination. *Chash* also is related to *chashah*, meaning "to be silent," suggesting a state of mind in which thought is quieted. Further, it is related to *chashmal*, an unusual term used in Ezekiel's famous chariot vision, which appears as a glow at the center of the form of a man (p. 109).

    The word *tummim*, with the connotation "perfections," hints that when a High Priest wore the *choshen* as one of the eight garments, he reached a level of perfection that made him a "twin"—*teomim*—to the Supernal Man that Ezekiel saw in his vision, which we will discuss below. See Van Dam, *op. cit.,* 141.

17. The prayer is inserted between the last two words of each verse of the blessing, while the *cohanim* chant a melody to give the congregation time to say the prayer. In other words, it is said between *Adonai* and *yishmerecha*; and between *eleicha* and *vichuneka*; some traditions also say the same prayer between *lecha* and *shalom*. Others insert a more general prayer for well being during the final verse between *lecha* and *shalom*.

18. Quoted in Elie Munk, *World of Prayer* Vol. II, 131.

Chapter 6

1. Buxbaum, *Jewish Spiritual Practices,* 554.

2. Luzzatto, *Way of God,* 191.

3. In the reports of dreams that appear in Louis Jacobs, *Jewish Mystical Testimonies* (New York: Schocken Books, 1977), we find only a few reports of a rabbi demanding or even consciously requesting something of a figure that appeared in his dream. The sages do not encourage attempts to control dreams. This is in contrast to the ego-centered efforts of many dream teachers in modern society who believe that "lucid dreaming" is a sign of proficiency in dreaming. On the contrary, we hold that

the more complete surrender of the ego opens the possibility of deeper dreaming—as most experts on mysticism have explained with regard to other forms of spiritual insight.

4. In addition, when a holy text comes to one's mouth upon arising, or one hears a child saying a biblical verse early in the morning, this is also considered a minor form of prophecy (*Berachot* 55b, 57b).

5. Zohar II:182b–183a, 200.

6. Zohar II:200a, 259.

7. Zohar II:199b, 258.

8. Rabbi Schneur Zalman of Liadi, *Hayom Yom for 27 Kislev, 5758* (December 26, 1997), and *Likutei Amarim: Tanya*, Chapter 29, 129. See also Buxbaum, *Jewish Spiritual Practices*, 547.

9. Zohar II:183b, 200.

10. Zohar II:200a, 259. Interestingly, people who have responsibility for a larger collectivity, such as a nation, may rise above what their level would otherwise be. For example, God permits kings to see more deeply than other people (Zohar II: 194b, 239). The Temple, when the *Shekhinah* dwelt there, was the source from which prophecy was drawn, and thus it was called the "Valley of Vision." The term *hizayon* (vision) has also been interpreted to signify "reflection of all the celestial hues" (Zohar II:203a, 270).

11. Zohar II:192a, 230. For example, what appears to be one dream may be segments, some of which apply to the dreamer, some to other people. Also, the Zohar says,

> Dreams are transmitted through the medium of Gabriel, who is the sixth in rank of inspiration; but a vision comes through the grade of the *chaya* that rules in the night. True, it says in one place, "Gabriel, make this man to understand the vision" (Daniel 8:16). The reason is that a dream is more precise than a vision, and may explain what is obscure in a vision, and therefore Gabriel was sent to explain to Daniel what was obscure in his vision. A "vision" is so called because it is like a mirror, in which all images are reflected (Zohar II:149b, 79).

> According to the Zohar, Jacob had his earlier Divine encounter, the dream of the ladder with angels going up and down on it, only in a dream because of his spiritual level at the time. He was not yet married, and he was not yet the head of the family because his father Isaac was still alive. But "when he came into the Holy Land with all the tribes, with the 'foundation of the house, the mother of the children rejoicing' we read, 'and God spoke to Israel in the visions of the night' (Genesis 46:2)—not 'dream,' but 'visions,' which are of another and higher grade."

> Similarly, when the Bible says of Solomon that "In Gibeon the Lord appeared

to him in a dream by night" (1 Kings 3:5), the words "appearing" and "dream" suggest a mixture of types. According to the Zohar, this was because Solomon had not then yet attained his full development. But later, when "God gave Solomon wisdom" (1 Kings 5:9) and "Solomon's wisdom excelled" (*v. 10*), "Solomon saw wisdom eye to eye and had no need of dreams. After he sinned, however, he was beholden again to dreams as before." Interestingly, the period when he did not need dreams is described the time when "the moon reached its fullness and the Temple was built," while when Solomon did not keep the covenant properly, it was called the time when "the moon began to wane." Zohar II:149b–150a, 80.

The Zohar's effort to clarify the levels of vision (a task that Maimonides also undertook) suggests the intense interest in varieties of spiritual experience in earlier centuries. For our purposes, however, it is enough to note the similarities between different kinds of dream-like experiences. Without claiming that dreams are prophetic, we do want to insist that they be taken seriously as sources of spiritual information, and are not merely allusions to individual psychological experiences.

12. This is mentioned briefly by Dov Noy in his Foreword to *Tales of Elijah the Prophet*, retold by Peninnah Schram (Northvale, N.J.: Jason Aronson, 1991), *xii*.

13. This higher world is the world of *tohu* (formlessness), which has a higher potential than our world (the world of *tikkun*), but also can manifest as confusion or evil. The reason that dreams often have elements that seem incongruous or confusing is because they have the quality of *tohu*. See *Torah Ohr, commentary on Parashat Miketz*. On the world of *tohu*, see Rabbi Aryeh Kaplan, *Inner Space: Introduction to Kabbalah, Meditation, and Prophecy,* edited by Abraham Sutton (Brooklyn: Moznaim, 1991), 82.

14. On twelve types of dreams, see Connie Kaplan, *A Woman's Book of Dreams* (Portland, Ore.: Beyond Words, 1999).

15. These *sefirot* are also the locus of desire for wealth, power, and sexuality. This is why prophets had to diminish their desires for physical pleasures, because if one used the energy of *Netzach* and *Hod* for physicality, these *sefirot* would not receive the non-physical information of prophecy.

Appendix C

1. The discussion is based on a verse in Proverbs: "Wisdom cries aloud in the street, she utters her voice in the broad places (1:20)" Zohar II 141b: 52–53.

Luzzatto discusses the importance of astrological influences in *Way of God,* 163: "Stars and planets serve as pipelines bringing influences from Heaven to the physical world. It was for this sake that the stars and planets were created. Every physical entity's existence is due to influences transmitted via stars and planets." Luzzatto explains that this information is limited and can always be altered by Divine intervention, which in turn is influenced by prayer. But astrology definitely does play a part, as he says: "This is what the prophet *Yeshayahu* [Isaiah] meant when he said, 'Now, let the astrologers, stargazers and fortune tellers stand up and tell you 'something' about what will come of you.'"

The Talmud also refers to constellations as having their own qualities, such as heat, cold, and healing abilities that affect the earth: "Were it not for the heat of Orion the world could not endure the cold of Pleiades, and were it not for the cold of Pleiades the world could not endure the heat of Orion. There is a tradition that were it not that the tail of the Scorpion has been placed in the Stream of Fire [probably the Milky Way], no one who has ever been stung by a scorpion could live." This is what is referred to in the words of the All-Merciful to Job: "Can you bind the chains of Pleiades or loose the bands of Orion? [Job 38:31]." Knowledge of astronomy was certainly valued; the sage Samuel said, "I am as familiar with the paths of heaven as with the streets of Nehardea, with the exception of the comet, about which I am ignorant" (*Berachot* 58b).

Glossary

Where appropriate, the literal meaning of the Hebrew is translated in quotation marks immediately after the word or phrase cited.

Ahavah: Love.

Amidah: "Standing." The prayer that culminates the daily Jewish services, said in a very quiet voice by each individual while standing, and then repeated by the cantor on behalf of the entire congregation.

Asiyah: The fourth and lowest of the Four Worlds according to Kabbalah, namely, the world of action and material form.

Baal Shem Tov: "Master of the Good Name." Israel ben Eliezer (1698–1760). The founder of Hasidism in Eastern Europe, famous for his tales, mystical feats, soul-travels, and parables explaining the Torah.

Bircat Cohanim: Priestly Blessing; also known as the Threefold Blessing, which originated in biblical times.

Chayah: The second of the five levels of the soul, involving a diminution of individual personality and the ability to sacrifice oneself for the greater good and ultimately for God.

Chayot: "Wild beasts" in popular usage, but in mysticism the winged beings with four faces that formed the Divine Chariot in the vision of Ezekiel 1.

Choshen: Breastplate of the High Priest, containing the *urim v'tummim*, and decorated with twelve stones representing the twelve tribes of Israel.

Cohain (plural, **cohanim**): "Priest." Historically, the segment of the tribe of Levi descended from Aaron and assigned to the most holy service in the wilderness Tabernacle and, later, the Temple in Jerusalem.

Devekut: "Clinging." A state of mystical elevation in which the practitioner achieves true closeness to God.

Echad: "One." The affirmation of the Oneness of God is basic to Jewish faith.

Gan Eden: "Garden of Eden." The original paradise of the Book of Genesis; also, the destination of the soul of a good person after death.

Hallel: A selection of psalms and phrases in praise of God recited after the *Amidah* on the new moon and most holidays.

Hamapil: "Who casts." The final prayer of the bedtime *Shema*, asking for illumination at night.

Hareni mochel: "I am ready to forgive." The forgiveness prayer. The name is derived, as with most Hebrew prayers, from its initial significant words.

Hashkivenu: "Lay us down." One of the prayers of the bedtime *Shema*, asking for protection during the night. It is imported from the evening synagogue service.

Halakhah: "The walking." The tradition of Jewish law.

Hasidism: A popular Jewish religious movement that began in eighteenth-century Eastern Europe, fully within the Orthodox framework, emphasizing devotion in prayer, love of one's fellow, and strong relationships between teacher (*rebbe*) and disciple (*hasid*). Hasidic masters were noted for their ability to transmit difficult mystical concepts to the ordinary person.

Havdalah: The home or synagogue ceremony that ends Shabbat, at least forty-two minutes after sunset on Saturday night. Fire created by a candle of more than one wick, spices, and wine are used in the ceremony.

Kabbalah: Generally, the Jewish mystical tradition. Its datable sources go back to the second century C.E., with important developments in the middle ages (e.g. the Zohar), the sixteenth century (Isaac Luria and other mystics of Sfat, Israel), and the late eighteenth and early nineteenth centuries (Hasidism).

Kavannah: "Intent." The inner focus to be cultivated when saying a prayer or performing a *mitzvah*.

Kelipot (singular, *kelipah*): "Husks." A term from Kabbalah signifying the evil forces in the world, which are portrayed as shells or husks that cover the sparks of Divine Light that are in every created being.

Levite: A descendant of the tribe of Levi. In Temple times, the Levites assisted the *cohanim*, cared for the appurtenances of the worship in the Temple, and sang accompaniments to the services.

Malkhut: "Kingship." The tenth of the *sefirot*, expressing the full manifestation of the soul in the material world.

Mezuzah: "Doorpost." A scroll, containing words of the *Shema*, that is affixed to the doors and gates of a Jewish home or business. Also, the case in which such a scroll is contained and protected.

Midrash: The general term for collections of homiletic and inspirational scriptural interpretation, particularly using stories and word-associations, produced in the third to eighth centuries C.E.

Mishnah: The primary written collection of rabbinic explanations of the laws of the Torah. Several "mishnahs" were collected in the late first and second centuries C.E., but the collection that became definitive was made by Rabbi Judah Ha-nasi toward the end of the second century. The Mishnah forms the core on which later Talmudic discussions (Gemara) are based. Both Mishnah and Gemara appear in any edition of the Talmud.

Nefesh: A biblical term for the soul, used in mystical writings to mean the aspect of the soul that vitalizes the physical body.

Neshamah: A biblical term for the soul, used in mystical writings to mean the aspect of soul most directly connected to the mind. Also, popularly, the essence of a person.

Ofanim: "Wheels." Angelic beings that bore the Divine Chariot seen by Ezekiel.

Ruach: A biblical term for the soul, usually translated as "spirit" and also meaning "wind." In mystical writings, *ruach* is the aspect of soul most closely connected with emotion and motivation.

Sefirot: (singular, *sefirah*): The ten Divine energies manifested in every process of creation.

Seraphim: Angelic beings of an intense, fiery appearance, seen in a vision of Isaiah.

Shema: "Hear." The first word of the major Jewish declaration of faith; also, the three paragraphs that constitute that declaration. It is a *mitzvah* to recite the *Shema* twice daily.

Shema al Mitah: "*Shema* on [one's] bed." The recital of the *Shema*, with accompanying prayers, including the *Hamapil*, that is performed at bedtime.

Shir Hashirim: "Song of Songs." Also known as Song of Solomon, this biblical love poem is a favorite of the mystics, who see it as an allegory of the love between God and the Jewish people.

Siddur: "Order." The Jewish prayerbook.

Sukkah: "Booth." The temporary structure, with roof made from branches, in which one eats and sleeps during the eight-day autumn holiday of Sukkot.

Tallit: "Prayer shawl." A ritual garment with four corners and fringes worn during the weekday morning prayers.

Talmud: The records of extensive discussions by Jewish sages on topics of Jewish law, from the third to sixth centuries, which form the central core of Judaism from that time onward. While Talmuds were collected and edited in both the Babylonian and Israelite communities, the word "Talmud" usually refers to the Babylonian Talmud (the other being the less comprehensive Jerusalem Talmud).

Tanach: An acronym for Torah, Prophets, and Writings (Torah, *Nevi'im*, and *Ketuvim*) that comprise the Hebrew Bible.

Tanya: "It has been taught." The first word and common title of the *Sefer Shel Benonim,* or "Book of the Average Person," written by Rabbi Schneur Zalman of Liadi at the beginning of the nineteenth century. It became a classic of Hasidic philosophy and practical teachings on prayer, not only for Rabbi Schneur Zalman's group, Chabad-Lubavitch, but for many other Hasidim as well. Today, it is universally recognized as a great work on spiritual self-improvement.

Tzara'at: A skin affliction described in the biblical Book of Leviticus. While its symptoms have sometimes been regarded as similar to leprosy, traditional Jewish interpretations hold that this was not a physical but a spiritual affliction particularly related to the sins of slander and gossip.

Tzitzit: Fringes attached to the ritual four-cornered garment (and, in ancient times, to any garment with four corners).

Urim vetummim: Oracular stones concealed in the *choshen,* or breastplate of the High Priest, enabling him to answer questions.

Yechidah: The highest of five levels of the soul, involving complete union with God.

Yichud Hashem: Unification of the name of God through prayer or ritual.

Zohar: A classic mystical text whose sources are claimed to go back to a famous second-century rabbi, Shimon bar Yochai. It was published and widely circulated beginning in the thirteenth century, and is the basis for most modern Jewish mysticism.

Recommended Readings

Buxbaum, Yitzhak. *Jewish Spiritual Practices*. Northvale, N.J.: Jason Aronson, 1990.

Frankiel, Tamar, and Judy Greenfeld. *Minding the Temple of the Soul: Balancing Body, Mind, and Spirit through Traditional Jewish Prayer, Movement, and Meditation*. Woodstock, Vt.: Jewish Lights, 1997.

Gillman, Neil. *The Death of Death: Resurrection and Immortality in Jewish Thought*. Woodstock, Vt.: Jewish Lights, 1997.

Gold, Avie, and Nosson Scherman, *Bircas Cohanim: The Priestly Blessings*. Brooklyn, N.Y.: Mesorah Publications, 1981.

Hoffman, Lawrence A. *My People's Prayer Book: Traditional Prayers, Modern Commentaries. Volume 1: The Sh'ma and Its Blessings*. Woodstock, Vt.: Jewish Lights, 1997.

Jacobs, Louis. *Jewish Mystical Testimonies*. New York: Schocken Books, 1977.

Kaplan, Connie Cockrell, *The Women's Book of Dreams: Dreaming as a Spiritual Practice*. Portland, Ore: Beyond Books, 1999.

Kushner, Lawrence. *God Was in This Place & I, i Did Not Know: Finding Self, Spirituality & Ultimate Meaning*. Woodstock, Vt.: Jewish Lights, 1991.

Lamm, Norman. *Shema: Law and Spirituality in Judaism*. New York: Jewish Publication Society, 1998.

Luzzatto, Moshe Chaim. *The Way of God*. New York: Feldheim, 1983.

Munk, Elie. *The World of Prayer*, 2 vols. New York: Feldheim, 1987.

Nachman of Breslov. *The Gentle Weapon: Prayers for Everyday and Not-So-Everyday Moments—Timeless Wisdom from the Teachings of the Hasidic Master, Rebbe Nachman of Breslov*. Adapted by Moshe Mykoff & S. C. Mizrahi with the Breslov Research Institute. Woodstock, Vt.: Jewish Lights, 1999.

Raphael, Simcha Paull. *Jewish Views of the Afterlife*. Northvale, N.J.: Jason Aronson, 1994.

Schneur Zalman of Liadi. *Likutei Amarim: Tanya*. Brooklyn, N.Y.: Kehot Publications, 1981.

Steinsaltz, Adin. *The Thirteen Petaled Rose*. Translated by Yehuda Hanegbi. New York: Basic Books, 1980.

Weisenthal, Simon. *The Sunflower*. New York: Schocken Books, 1994.

About JEWISH LIGHTS Publishing

People of all faiths and backgrounds yearn for books that attract, engage, educate and spiritually inspire.

Our principal goal is to stimulate thought and help all people learn about who the Jewish People are, where they come from, and what the future can be made to hold. While people of our diverse Jewish heritage are the primary audience, our books speak to people in the Christian world as well and will broaden their understanding of Judaism and the roots of their own faith.

We bring to you authors who are at the forefront of spiritual thought and experience. While each has something different to say, they all say it in a voice that you can hear.

Our books are designed to welcome you and then to engage, stimulate and inspire. We judge our success not only by whether or not our books are beautiful and commercially successful, but by whether or not they make a difference in your life.

We at Jewish Lights take great care to produce beautiful books that present meaningful spiritual content in a form that reflects the art of making high quality books. Therefore, we want to acknowledge those who contributed to the production of this book.

Stuart M. Matlins

Stuart M. Matlins, Publisher

PRODUCTION
Marian B. Wallace & Bridgett Taylor

EDITORIAL
Sandra Korinchak, Emily Wichland,
Martha McKinney & Amanda Dupuis

COVER DESIGN
Jan Martí, Command Z, Palo Alto, California

INTERIOR TYPESETTING
Ronnie Serr, Alphabet House, Los Angeles, California

TEXT DESIGN
Chelsea Dippel, Chelsea Designs, Scotia, New York

COVER PRINTING
John P. Pow Company, South Boston, Massachusetts

TEXT PRINTING AND BINDING
Hamilton Printing, Rensselaer, New York

Spirituality

The Women's Torah Commentary: *New Insights from Women Rabbis on the 54 Weekly Torah Portions* Ed. by *Rabbi Elyse Goldstein*

For the first time, women rabbis provide a commentary on the entire Torah. More than 25 years after the first woman was ordained a rabbi in America, women have an impressive group of spiritual role models that they never had before. Here, in a week-by-week format, these inspiring teachers bring their rich perspectives to bear on the biblical text. A perfect gift for others, or for yourself. 6 x 9, 432 pp, HC, ISBN 1-58023-076-8 **$29.95**

Bringing the Psalms to Life
How to Understand and Use the Book of Psalms by *Rabbi Daniel F. Polish*

Here, the most beloved—and least understood—of the books in the Bible comes alive. This simultaneously insightful and practical guide shows how the psalms address a myriad of spiritual issues in our lives: feeling abandoned, overcoming illness, dealing with anger, and more. 6 x 9, 208 pp, HC, ISBN 1-58023-077-6 **$21.95**

Stepping Stones to Jewish Spiritual Living: *Walking the Path*
Morning, Noon, and Night by *Rabbi James L. Mirel* & *Karen Bonnell Werth*

Transforms our daily routine into sacred acts of mindfulness. Chapters are arranged according to the cycle of each day. "A wonderful, practical, and inspiring guidebook to gently bring the riches of Jewish practice into our busy, everyday lives. Highly recommended." —*Rabbi David A. Cooper.* 6 x 9, 240 pp, Quality PB, ISBN 1-58023-074-1 **$16.95**; HC, ISBN 1-58023-003-2 **$21.95**

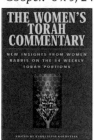 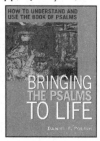 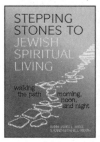 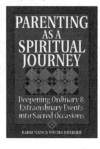 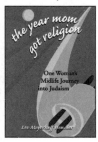

Parenting As a Spiritual Journey:
Deepening Ordinary & Extraordinary Events into Sacred Occasions
by Rabbi Nancy Fuchs-Kreimer 6 x 9, 224 pp, Quality PB, ISBN 1-58023-016-4 **$16.95**

The Year Mom Got Religion: *One Woman's Midlife Journey into Judaism*
by Lee Meyerhoff Hendler 6 x 9, 208 pp, Quality PB, ISBN 1-58023-070-9 **$15.95**;
HC, ISBN 1-58023-000-8 **$19.95**

Moses—The Prince, the Prophet: *His Life, Legend & Message for Our Lives*
by Rabbi Levi Meier, Ph.D. 6 x 9, 224 pp, Quality PB, ISBN 1-58023-069-5 **$16.95**;
HC, ISBN 1-58023-013-X **$23.95**

Ancient Secrets: *Using the Stories of the Bible to Improve Our Everyday Lives*
by Rabbi Levi Meier, Ph.D. 5½ x 8½, 288 pp, Quality PB, ISBN 1-58023-064-4 **$16.95**

Or phone, fax or mail to: **JEWISH LIGHTS Publishing**
Sunset Farm Offices, Route 4 • P.O. Box 237 • Woodstock, Vermont 05091
Tel: (802) 457-4000 • Fax: (802) 457-4004 • www.jewishlights.com
Credit card orders: (800) **962-4544** (9AM–5PM ET Monday–Friday)
Generous discounts on quantity orders. SATISFACTION GUARANTEED. Prices subject to change.

Children's Spirituality

God Said Amen
by *Sandy Eisenberg Sasso*
Full-color illus. by *Avi Katz*

For ages 4 & up

MULTICULTURAL, NONDENOMINATIONAL, NONSECTARIAN

A warm and inspiring tale of two kingdoms: Midnight Kingdom is overflowing with water but has no oil to light its lamps; Desert Kingdom is blessed with oil but has no water to grow its gardens. The kingdoms' rulers ask God for help but are too stubborn to ask each other. It takes a minstrel, a pair of royal riding-birds and their young keepers, and a simple act of kindness to show that they need only reach out to each other to find God's answer to their prayers.

9 x 12, 32 pp, HC, Full-color illus., ISBN 1-58023-080-6 **$16.95**

For Heaven's Sake
by *Sandy Eisenberg Sasso*; Full-color illus. by *Kathryn Kunz Finney*

For ages 4 & up

MULTICULTURAL, NONDENOMINATIONAL, NONSECTARIAN

Everyone talked about heaven: "Thank heavens." "Heaven forbid." "For heaven's sake, Isaiah." But no one would say what heaven was or how to find it. So Isaiah decides to find out, by seeking answers from many different people. "This book is a reminder of how well Sandy Sasso knows the minds of children. But it may surprise—and delight—readers to find how well she knows us grown-ups too." —*Maria Harris*, National Consultant in Religious Education, and author of *Teaching and Religious Imagination* 9 x 12, 32 pp, HC, Full-color illus., ISBN 1-58023-054-7 **$16.95**

But God Remembered: Stories of Women from Creation to the Promised Land
by *Sandy Eisenberg Sasso*; Full-color illus. by *Bethanne Andersen*

For ages 8 & up

NONDENOMINATIONAL, NONSECTARIAN

A fascinating collection of four different stories of women only briefly mentioned in biblical tradition and religious texts. Award-winning author Sasso vibrantly brings to life courageous and strong women from ancient tradition; all teach important values through their actions and faith. "Exquisite. . . . A book of beauty, strength and spirituality." —*Association of Bible Teachers* 9 x 12, 32 pp, HC, Full-color illus., ISBN 1-879045-43-5 **$16.95**

God in Between
by *Sandy Eisenberg Sasso*; Full-color illus. by *Sally Sweetland*

For ages 4 & up

MULTICULTURAL, NONDENOMINATIONAL, NONSECTARIAN

If you wanted to find God, where would you look? A magical, mythical tale that teaches that God can be found where we are: within all of us and the relationships between us. "This happy and wondrous book takes our children on a sweet and holy journey into God's presence." —*Rabbi Wayne Dosick, Ph.D.*, author of *Golden Rules* and *Soul Judaism*
9 x 12, 32 pp, HC, Full-color illus., ISBN 1-879045-86-9 **$16.95**

Life Cycle

Jewish Paths toward Healing and Wholeness
A Personal Guide to Dealing with Suffering
by *Rabbi Kerry M. Olitzky*

"Why me?" Why do we suffer? How can we heal? Grounded in the spiritual traditions of Judaism, this book provides healing rituals, psalms and prayers that help readers initiate a dialogue with God, to guide them along the complicated path of healing and wholeness.
6 x 9, 192 pp, Quality PB, ISBN 1-58023-068-7 **$15.95**   (Avail. Aug. 2000)

Mourning & Mitzvah: *A Guided Journal for Walking the Mourner's Path through Grief to Healing*
by *Anne Brener*, L.C.S.W.; Foreword by *Rabbi Jack Riemer*; Intro. by *Rabbi William Cutter*

For those who mourn a death, for those who would help them, for those who face a loss of any kind, Brener teaches us the power and strength available to us in the fully experienced mourning process. 7½ x 9, 288 pp, Quality PB, ISBN 1-879045-23-0 **$19.95**

Tears of Sorrow, Seeds of Hope
A Jewish Spiritual Companion for Infertility and Pregnancy Loss
by *Rabbi Nina Beth Cardin*

A spiritual companion that enables us to mourn infertility, a lost pregnancy, or a stillbirth within the prayers, rituals, and meditations of Judaism. By drawing on the texts of tradition, it creates readings and rites of mourning, and through them provides a wellspring of compassion, solace—and hope. 6 x 9, 192 pp, HC, ISBN 1-58023-017-2 **$19.95**

Lifecycles
V. 1: *Jewish Women on Life Passages & Personal Milestones* AWARD WINNER!
Ed. and with Intros. by Rabbi Debra Orenstein
V. 2: *Jewish Women on Biblical Themes in Contemporary Life* AWARD WINNER!
Ed. and with Intros. by Rabbi Debra Orenstein and Rabbi Jane Rachel Litman
V. 1: 6 x 9, 480 pp, Quality PB, ISBN 1-58023-018-0 **$19.95**; HC, ISBN 1-879045-14-1 **$24.95**
V. 2: 6 x 9, 464 pp, Quality PB, ISBN 1-58023-019-9 **$19.95**; HC, ISBN 1-879045-15-X **$24.95**

Grief in Our Seasons: *A Mourner's Kaddish Companion*
by Rabbi Kerry M. Olitzky 4½ x 6½, 448 pp, Quality PB, ISBN 1-879045-55-9 **$15.95**

A Time to Mourn, A Time to Comfort: *A Guide to Jewish Bereavement and Comfort*
by Dr. Ron Wolfson 7 x 9, 336 pp, Quality PB, ISBN 1-879045-96-6 **$16.95**

When a Grandparent Dies
A Kid's Own Remembering Workbook for Dealing with Shiva and the Year Beyond
by Nechama Liss-Levinson, Ph.D.
8 x 10, 48 pp, HC, Illus., 2-color text, ISBN 1-879045-44-3 **$15.95**

So That Your Values Live On: *Ethical Wills & How to Prepare Them*
Ed. by Rabbi Jack Riemer & Professor Nathaniel Stampfer
6 x 9, 272 pp, Quality PB, ISBN 1-879045-34-6 **$17.95**

Spirituality

My People's Prayer Book: *Traditional Prayers, Modern Commentaries*
Ed. by *Dr. Lawrence A. Hoffman*

This momentous, critically-acclaimed series is truly a people's prayer book, one that provides a diverse and exciting commentary to the traditional liturgy. It will help modern men and women find new wisdom and guidance in Jewish prayer, and bring liturgy into their lives. Each book includes Hebrew text, modern translation, and commentaries *from all perspectives* of the Jewish world. Vol. 1—*The Sh'ma and Its Blessings,* 7 x 10, 168 pp, HC, ISBN 1-879045-79-6 **$23.95**
Vol. 2—*The Amidah,* 7 x 10, 240 pp, HC, ISBN 1-879045-80-X **$23.95**
Vol. 3—*P'sukei D'zimrah* (Morning Psalms), 7 x 10, 240 pp, HC, ISBN 1-879045-81-8 **$23.95**
Vol. 4—*Seder K'riyat Hatorah* (Shabbat Torah Service), 7 x 10, 240 pp, ISBN 1-879045-82-6 **$23.95**
(Avail. Sept. 2000)

Voices from Genesis: *Guiding Us through the Stages of Life*
by *Dr. Norman J. Cohen*

In a brilliant blending of modern *midrash* (finding contemporary meaning from biblical texts) and the life stages of Erik Erikson's developmental psychology, the characters of Genesis come alive to give us insights for our own journeys. 6 x 9, 192 pp, HC, ISBN 1-879045-75-3 **$21.95**

   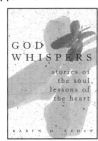 

God Whispers: *Stories of the Soul, Lessons of the Heart*
by Rabbi Karyn D. Kedar 6 x 9, 176 pp, Quality PB, ISBN 1-58023-088-1 **$15.95**;
HC, ISBN 1-58023-023-7 **$19.95**

Being God's Partner: *How to Find the Hidden Link Between Spirituality and Your Work*
by Rabbi Jeffrey K. Salkin; Intro. by Norman Lear AWARD WINNER!
6 x 9, 192 pp, Quality PB, ISBN 1-879045-65-6 **$16.95**; HC, ISBN 1-879045-37-0 **$19.95**

ReVisions: *Seeing Torah through a Feminist Lens* AWARD WINNER!
by Rabbi Elyse Goldstein 5½ x 8½, 208 pp, HC, ISBN 1-58023-047-4 **$19.95**

Soul Judaism: *Dancing with God into a New Era*
by Rabbi Wayne Dosick 5½ x 8½, 304 pp, Quality PB, ISBN 1-58023-053-9 **$16.95**

Finding Joy: *A Practical Spiritual Guide to Happiness* AWARD WINNER!
by Rabbi Dannel I. Schwartz with Mark Hass
6 x 9, 192 pp, Quality PB, ISBN 1-58023-009-1 **$14.95**; HC, ISBN 1-879045-53-2 **$19.95**

The Empty Chair: *Finding Hope and Joy—*
Timeless Wisdom from a Hasidic Master, Rebbe Nachman of Breslov AWARD WINNER!
Adapted by Moshe Mykoff and the Breslov Research Institute
4 x 6, 128 pp, Deluxe PB, 2-color text, ISBN 1-879045-67-2 **$9.95**

The Gentle Weapon: *Prayers for Everyday and Not-So-Everyday Moments*
Adapted from the Wisdom of Rebbe Nachman of Breslov by Moshe Mykoff and
S. C. Mizrahi, with the Breslov Research Institute
4 x 6, 144 pp, Deluxe PB, 2-color text, ISBN 1-58023-022-9 **$9.95**

"Who Is a Jew?" *Conversations, Not Conclusions* by Meryl Hyman
6 x 9, 272 pp, Quality PB, ISBN 1-58023-052-0 **$16.95**; HC, ISBN 1-879045-76-1 **$23.95**

The Way Into... Series

A major 14-volume series to be completed over the next several years, *The Way Into...* provides an accessible and usable "guided tour" of the Jewish faith, its people, its history and beliefs—in total, an introduction to Judaism for adults that will enable them to understand and interact with sacred texts.

Each volume is written by a major modern scholar and teacher, and is organized around an important concept of Judaism.

The Way Into... will enable all readers to achieve a real sense of Jewish cultural literacy through guided study. Forthcoming volumes include:

 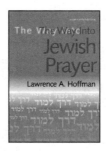  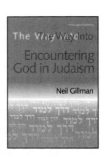

The Way Into Torah

by *Dr. Norman J. Cohen*

What is "Torah"? What are the different approaches to studying Torah? What are the different levels of understanding Torah? For whom is the study intended? Explores the origins and development of Torah, why it should be studied and how to do it. Addresses these and many other issues in this easy-to-use, easy-to-understand introduction to the ancient subject.

6 x 9, 160 pp, HC, ISBN 1-58023-028-8 **$21.95**

The Way Into Jewish Prayer

by *Dr. Lawrence A. Hoffman*

Explores the reasons for and the ways of Jewish prayer. Opens the door to 3,000 years of the Jewish way to God by making available all you need to feel at home in Jewish worship. Provides basic definitions of the terms you need to know as well as thoughtful analysis of the depth that lies beneath Jewish prayer.

6 x 9, 160 pp, HC, ISBN 1-58023-027-X **$21.95**

The Way Into Jewish Mystical Tradition

by *Rabbi Lawrence Kushner*

Explains the principles of Jewish mystical thinking, their religious and spiritual significance, and how they relate to our lives. A book that allows us to experience and understand the Jewish mystical approach to our place in the world.

6 x 9, 176 pp, HC, ISBN 1-58023-029-6 **$21.95** (Avail. Sept. 2000)

The Way Into Encountering God in Judaism

by *Dr. Neil Gillman*

Explains how Jews have encountered God throughout history—and today—by exploring the many metaphors for God in Jewish tradition. Explores the Jewish tradition's passionate but also conflicting ways of relating to God as Creator, relational partner, and a force in history and nature.

6 x 9, 176 pp, HC, ISBN 1-58023-025-3 **$21.95** (Avail. Sept. 2000)

Spirituality & More

These Are the Words: *A Vocabulary of Jewish Spiritual Life*

by *Arthur Green*

What are the most essential ideas, concepts and terms that an educated person needs to know about Judaism? From *Adonai* (My Lord) to *zekhut* (merit), this enlightening and entertaining journey through Judaism teaches us the 149 core Hebrew words that constitute the basic vocabulary of Jewish spiritual life. 6 x 9, 304 pp, HC, ISBN 1-58023-024-5 **$21.95**

The Enneagram and Kabbalah: *Reading Your Soul*

by *Rabbi Howard A. Addison*

Combines two of the most powerful maps of consciousness known to humanity—The Tree of Life (the *Sefirot*) from the Jewish mystical tradition of *Kabbalah*, and the nine-pointed Enneagram—and shows how, together, they can provide a powerful tool for self-knowledge, critique, and transformation. 6 x 9, 176 pp, Quality PB, ISBN 1-58023-001-6 **$15.95**

Embracing the Covenant
Converts to Judaism Talk About Why & How

Ed. and with Intros. by *Rabbi Allan L. Berkowitz* and *Patti Moskovitz*

Through personal experiences of 20 converts to Judaism, this book illuminates reasons for converting, the quest for a satisfying spirituality, the appeal of the Jewish tradition and how conversion has changed lives—the convert's, and the lives of those close to them.
6 x 9, 192 pp, Quality PB, ISBN 1-879045-50-8 **$15.95**

 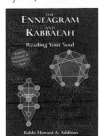   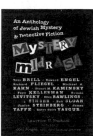

Shared Dreams: *Martin Luther King, Jr. and the Jewish Community*
by Rabbi Marc Schneier; Preface by Martin Luther King III
6 x 9, 240 pp, HC, ISBN 1-58023-062-8 **$24.95**

Mystery Midrash: *An Anthology of Jewish Mystery & Detective Fiction*
Ed. by Lawrence W. Raphael; Preface by Joel Siegel, ABC's *Good Morning America*
6 x 9, 304 pp, Quality PB, ISBN 1-58023-055-5 **$16.95**

The Jewish Gardening Cookbook: *Growing Plants & Cooking for Holidays & Festivals*
by Michael Brown 6 x 9, 224 pp, HC, Illus., ISBN 1-58023-004-0 **$21.95**

Wandering Stars: *An Anthology of Jewish Fantasy & Science Fiction* Ed. by Jack Dann; Intro. by Isaac Asimov 6 x 9, 272 pp, Quality PB, ISBN 1-58023-005-9 **$16.95**

More Wandering Stars
An Anthology of Outstanding Stories of Jewish Fantasy and Science Fiction
Ed. by Jack Dann; Intro. by Isaac Asimov 6 x 9, 192 pp, Quality PB, ISBN 1-58023-063-6 **$16.95**

A Heart of Wisdom: *Making the Jewish Journey from Midlife through the Elder Years*
Ed. by Susan Berrin; Foreword by Harold Kushner
6 x 9, 384 pp, Quality PB, ISBN 1-58023-051-2 **$18.95**; HC, ISBN 1-879045-73-7 **$24.95**

Sacred Intentions: *Daily Inspiration to Strengthen the Spirit, Based on Jewish Wisdom*
by Rabbi Kerry M. Olitzky and Rabbi Lori Forman
4½ x 6½, 448 pp, Quality PB, ISBN 1-58023-061-X **$15.95**

Discovering *Jewish Meditation*

Instruction & **ual Practice**

by *Nan Fink Ge*

Gives readers of a   of Jewish meditation
on your own, start   nnection to God and
to greater insight a   067-9 **$16.95**

Meditation fr **ers Share**

Their Practices,

A "how-to" guide fo   on the wisdom of
22 masters of medita   iled compendium
of the experts' "best   56 pp, Quality PB,
ISBN 1-58023-049-0 **$**

The Way of Flam

A Guide to the Fo **ation**

by *Avram Davis* 4½ x

Entering the Temple **Jewish Prayers, Movements, and**
Meditations for the End of the Day by *Tamar Frankiel* and *Judy Greenfeld*
Nighttime spirituality is much more than bedtime prayers! Here, you'll uncover deeper
meaning to familiar nighttime prayers—and learn to combine the prayers with movements
and meditations to enhance your physical and psychological well-being.
7 x 10, 192 pp, Quality PB, Illus., ISBN 1-58023-079-2 **$16.95**

Minding the Temple of the Soul: *Balancing Body, Mind, and Spirit*
through Traditional Jewish Prayer, Movement, and Meditation

by *Tamar Frankiel* and *Judy Greenfeld*

This new spiritual approach to physical health introduces readers to a spiritual tradition that
affirms the body and enables them to reconceive their bodies in a more positive light. Focuses on
traditional Jewish prayers, with exercises, movements, and meditations. 7 x 10, 184 pp, Quality PB,
Illus., ISBN 1-879045-64-8 **$16.95**; Audiotape of the Blessings, Movements and Meditations (60-min.
cassette), JN01 **$9.95**; Videotape of the Movements and Meditations (46-min. VHS), S507 **$20.00**

Or phone, fax or mail to: **JEWISH LIGHTS Publishing**
Sunset Farm Offices, Route 4 • P.O. Box 237 • Woodstock, Vermont 05091
Tel: (802) 457-4000 • Fax: (802) 457-4004 • www.jewishlights.com
Credit card orders (800) 962-4544 (9AM–5PM ET Monday–Friday)
Generous discounts on quantity orders. SATISFACTION GUARANTEED. Prices subject to change.